Faces People Wear

FACES PEOPLE WEAR

by

CHARLES DI SALVO

with

CLAIRE COX

HAWTHORN BOOKS, INC.

Publishers   New York

FACES PEOPLE WEAR

First Edition: 1968

1144

ACKNOWLEDGMENTS

The authors wish to thank the following for permission to quote
previously published material:

Edrita Fried, *The Ego in Love and Sexuality;* copyright 1960. Grune
& Stratton, Inc.; used by permission of the publishers.

Social Action (published by the Council for Christian Social Action
of the United Church of Christ) for quotations from the issue devoted
to "Civil Liberties and Homosexuality" (December, 1967).

To Sonya

Contents

Introduction

"Who are you?" This question is receiving a great deal of attention these days. All of us are constantly faced with a need to define ourselves—our state of being—and to act out that definition in our relationships with others.

The need for self-examination and definition seems more acute today than ever before. With fewer external certainties on which to hang the hat of our "identity," we are forced to turn inward for our answers.

My original training was as a clergyman, and in the early pursuit of this profession I noticed how many people were seeking to work out the questions of their identity, meaning, and worth through religion. Some used this approach more wisely than others. Some misused it or used it to deny their true state of being.

As I worked with people involved in the quandaries that the question of identity poses, I became increasingly aware of the limited tools provided in theological training to enable the clergyman to deal with this crucial matter. Yet, the identity question is one the minister cannot ignore, personally or professionally, if he is to be conscientious in his work.

This concern led me to a study of the techniques of psychotherapy. In my work as a pastoral counselor, psychotherapist, and consultant, I constantly find people trying to deal with the question of their own state of being. Often they are frightened, not only by the enormousness and constancy of the task, but also by their lack of ability to understand the identity question as a normal one in human existence and experience.

After writing an editorial on the question "Who Am I?" in a professional journal some years ago, I began to think more and more of the possibility of presenting to the layman a systematic illustration of the way the question of identity confronts man and, in turn, is faced by him from childhood through old age.

As an experiment, I began asking my friends and clients, "Who are you?" The answers I received indicated that most people are in an identity quandary to some degree. In the groups with which I work, I began to ask the question to see how people deal with it. Here is an illustration of how some of the groups reacted to the question.

"Who are you?" I asked the dark-haired, tense young man seated at my left.

He appeared startled at the question.

"You know very well who I am," he replied. "I'm a computer programmer."

"Oh, I see," I commented. "You are your *job*. Is that right?"

I turned then to the attractive middle-aged woman sitting next to him.

"And who are *you?*"

She hesitated a moment and said, "I'm Mary Jones, of course."

"And *you* are your *name,* or at least that is your impression of yourself, isn't it?" I asked.

So it went, around the circle of men and women.

One participant, when asked who he was, blurted, "I'm a *man,*" and the fellow next to him expanded on this in reference to himself by declaring, "I'm a *white* man."

"You mean you are your sex, your gender?" I said to the first, and to the second, "You feel that your color as well as your sex is what gives you your sense of being?"

The computer expert was warming to the game by this time and volunteered: "I've got it now! I'm a thirty-four-year-old white man. I'm in a very important job feeding information into computers. I help my company do its job better, faster, and more efficiently. I'm married and have three children. I live in a twelve-room house in suburbia. Now if that doesn't tell you who I am, I just don't know what to say."

"It does not really tell me what I want to know," I responded. "It has told me a lot *about* you, but really it doesn't give me much feeling as to who *you* are."

"Well, then," he said in a slightly querulous tone, "I guess I just don't understand what you mean when you ask, 'Who are you?' "

"What do you think I mean?" I replied.

"I give up. You tell me who I am if you are so smart."

Responses of this kind were made so often by so many that I proceeded to write a book for the layman to try to help him recognize that he, too, *might* have an identity problem and then to suggest some answers to his questions and ways in which he might learn to cope with his own quandaries and those of others.

This book is meant as an *illustration* of the various faces of identity people wear at different stages of their lives. Because it is an illustration, it is not meant to be an exhaustive study of identity. As the reader proceeds, he will note that some of the examples are pathological in nature, but many are not. The basic facts of each illustration are correct, but the details of some of the cases have been changed to preserve anonymity.

It is my hope that presenting this illustration for the layman will help him to become less anxious as he faces the question of his own identity—and more tolerant and understanding of the way others are trying to deal with their search for answers to the question: Who are *you?*

CHARLES DI SALVO

1

Who Are You—Really?

The crisis of identity is one of the principal problems beset-
ting our increasingly troubled society. Put in the simplest possible terms, many of us do not know who we really are. Some
of us are struggling with the problem, trying to penetrate the
maze of experience in order to find ourselves. Most people
probably are unaware that the problem exists—if you asked
them who they were, they would not know what you were
talking about.

All around us we can see sharp—even harsh—evidence that
more and more people are floundering. The high and still soar-
ing rates of juvenile delinquency, suicide, divorce, alcoholism,
narcotics addiction, and mental breakdown directly or indirectly affect the lives of millions of people. Rebellious teen-
agers are thrashing about blindly in an effort to find a niche for
themselves in a society they consider lacking in compassion,
ruthless or even vicious. College students unprepared to take

their place in an uncertain, war-threatened world try to expand their egos with LSD and psychedelic posters. Parents are themselves so confused that they can offer little guidance. Ghetto dwellers with little or no sense of self-worth rampage in riots that undermine the very programs that would enable them to break the old chains of poverty and ignorance.

The computer programmer has become so closely identified with his machine that he thinks of himself more as an automaton than as a human being. Atomic scientists have become "authorities" on everything, omnipotent in their own eyes, because they helped create man's deadliest weapon. Young college graduates, angry and puzzled because they cannot start in high-paying, titled jobs, have rather inadequate ideas of their worth. Housewives, mothers, mechanics, ministers, and corporation executives—all of us—are caught up in the identity crisis.

There probably is not a group in our society today that is more lost than the hippies and other runaways. They have found a superficial kind of identity with other youngsters by hiding behind professions of love for their fellowman, whom they really probably loathe, and by appearing in the uniform of long, dirty hair and sloppy apparel. These youngsters have been plunged into a terrifying identity crisis.

Two other extremes come to mind. One is the person who deals with today's crisis next week or next year by living on credit. He never catches up, and he has a hard time tracking down his identity because of his constant striving for material things on a buy-status-now, pay-later basis. At the other extreme is the person whose identity is so threatened that he buries himself in security. He may hold a civil service job for his entire working life. This is particularly true of Americans who entered the civil service during the Great Depression and stuck to it even when they could have found higher-paying and more interesting work when prosperity returned. This was emphasized in the late 1960's, when many of these workers reached retirement age, producing a shortage, for people with their talents and abilities were spurning the steady security of being on the government payroll in a time of prosperity. Men often enlist in the Army for security; women enter teaching, with its tenure and pensions, for the same reason. And, interestingly, chronic criminals who spend more time in prison than out also may be looking for their own peculiar kind of security. All are wandering through the identity gap.

The life question of "Who am I?" becomes a "game" in which some people are so involved that, for example, the busy executive "forgets" to go home—forgets his family because he is so immersed in his job that he has become completely identified with it. Our jails and mental hospitals are filled with people who have never found out who they are, or perhaps never tried to find out—or simply did not care to know. The men and women who stretch out every week on analysts' couches are there because they are desperately involved in the search for their own identities.

Increasingly, when we pick up a newspaper or a magazine, switch on the television set, or attend a play or a movie, there is reference to the identity crisis. The recent hit movie *The Graduate* has as its central theme a young man's effort to find out who he is and what he wants to be. *Spofford*, a Broadway success of 1968, deals with the quest for identity by residents of an affluent suburb of New York City. An egghead religious magazine, *Colloquy,* carried a long article called "Liturgy of Identity." The film *Luther* was characterized by a critic writing in *Saturday Review* as being in actuality more a search for identity on the part of the playwright than the story of the Protestant Reformation.

Being able to see and yet not perceive seems to be one of the characteristics of our generation, at least where oneself is concerned. To understand how little thought we give to the question of our true identities, walk down any street and watch the people approaching you. Note how many of them seem oblivious to what is going on around them. Why should this be, at a time in history when people are supposed to be more alert and observant than ever? The reason for this seeming unawareness of what is going on may be that people are finding life a terrifying experience; they are trying to protect themselves by hiding from the anxieties they encounter in the everyday world. Rather than face these anxieties, which result from trying to come to grips with such questions as that of identity, they plod on, looking neither to left nor right, never even wondering where they fit into the scheme of things.

Why is this estrangement from self so prevalent today? Why was it not so much a problem in past generations? Certainly not because it was an easier question to deal with in times gone by. Perhaps it was a question people did not have to answer to any great extent. Today the changing role of women, of the family and marriage and the community, and of the world of technology are all factors in the identity crisis. It is much more difficult to establish one's identity today than it was even fifty or seventy-five years ago. Life's pace was slower then. More important, it was easier not to have to face the question of identity at all, since people often lived and died in the same place and cultural setting in which they were born. This made it easier for them to assume hand-me-down identities and value systems.

Today, as we pick up and move about so freely, far from our grandfathers' roots, we become more acutely aware that to assume the mantle of our grandfathers' identity for ourselves makes little sense and does not speak to the needs of our lifetime. Principles of self-definition that were acceptable in previous generations just do not fit today, with the result that vast numbers of us simply have not been able to find out who we are. When we insist on defining ourselves by what we *do,* we tend to *become* what we do, and when our jobs are threatened, we then are threatened as persons. You can see the kind of chaos this places us in when you consider, say, the computer programmer, or a teletype operator, whose job requires a certain amount of skill and carries a degree of status within an organization. Suppose that tomorrow something was developed by the computer programmer—who may be having identity problems himself—that eliminated the need for teletype operators. For the man whose identity derived from his work this would be a crisis, for his concept of self would be undermined.

If identification with job is strong enough, a man can become anxious, frightened, and perhaps even desperate. Since "teletype operator" no longer exists, he may have a feeling that *he* does not exist either or that he is not much of a person anymore. He may have a difficult time in training for or becoming attuned to a new type of work. He may even be plunged into emotional disorder.

Indeed, automation is accentuating the entire matter of "Who am I?" The creation of machines that can do man's work—and even his thinking—becomes a threat to the people who derived so much of their sense of being from their workaday functions. Two problems result: One, they are out of a job and all their emotional "fringe benefits" are gone, and, two, they now find that they are comparing themselves with a piece of metal, a machine. This can be very denigrating. Egos are further sapped by other kinds of depersonalization in business and industry that have turned people into numbers.

An engineer I know weathered a job crisis very well. During the Depression he could not find anything in his field. He had a wife and four children to support, so he took what he could get—a job as an iceman. Just as he had not been faced with the problem of identifying himself with his job as an engineer, neither did he identify himself as an iceman. Early in World War II he found an engineering job and is prominent in his field today. He came as close as anyone I have known personally to having a sense of his identity. He was *himself,* regardless of the nature of his job.

One of the best examples of this kind of identity quandary I know is the minister who is so engrossed in his calling that he has no friends outside the church and never does anything unrelated to his work. He goes so far as to feel that he cannot take time off because the world cannot exist without his services. Another minister friend declined an invitation to a party at our home because "something might come up in the parish that would require my presence."

Some years back, when I was an Army chaplain, a chaplain for whom I worked displayed a poor sense of identity. He took a leave only when forced to, for he could not tolerate being away from his post. When he finally agreed to a leave, he simply could not find himself. At 10 A.M. the day after he left, he came into the office explaining, "I forgot my hat." The next morning he came in again, this time giving the excuse that "I need a book from my office." He visited the office twenty-eight out of the thirty days of his leave on one pretext or another. A lost man when he was not behind his desk, he did not know who he was.

In my own work as a psychotherapist, I find that the people who turn up in my office are most frequently confronted with a crisis concerning their own identity. After a brief period, I usually ask: "Who are you?" It is surprising how often this simple question makes people anxious and frustrated. It makes some people so anxious, in fact, that they cannot cope with their lack of self-knowledge, so they run away from counseling that could help them. Fortunately, a gratifying number do stay and grapple with the question, often arriving at satisfactory answers.

There are times when the identity question arouses resentment, as was the case with a minister I counseled for several months. He came to me because the "pressures" of his job were becoming unbearable; working in the labors of the Lord was so demanding that he had no time for anything else. I found this impossible to believe, so I very carefully analyzed with him how he spent his time on one particular day. As the hours unfolded, I noted that he included in what he considered his church work several errands that appeared to be personal. For example, he told me he went to the store. When I asked about this, he said it was a personal matter. I inquired

how he could consider this a part of his job. He found it difficult to understand why I even raised the question; he was so
closely identified with his work and had answered his own
question of identity so thoroughly in terms of it that he was
unable to see where his job ended and his personal life began.

Most of us probably have learned in one way or another to
think about ourselves in terms of some expression of our identity. This is an evasion, deliberate or otherwise, of the need to
look ourselves fully in the face. It is much easier to think of
ourselves in terms of our sex or our job or our relationships
to our family or to the community. By doing so, we feel more
comfortable because it spares us from wrestling with the deeper
question of who we *really* are.

Every period of our lives, from the cradle to the grave,
poses a new set of problems for us. How we survive and solve
these problems depends on us as individuals as well as on
those with whom we live and associate. While the various
problems have different kinds of solutions, there really is only
one "right" answer to the question "Who am I?"

The final answer is simple, and at the same time very complex.

It is: *"I am me!"*

The person who can say, *"I am me,"* and understands on
an emotional level what he means, begins to know *who* he is.

"I am *myself*," he will say, "the only person of this particular kind, who is involved in the interpersonal world in these
ways . . . but who feels this way and that way." The key, however, is: *I am me! There is nobody else like me!*

A story about a father and his eight-year-old daughter illus-
trates this. As he tucked her into bed one night, the little girl

suddenly said, "Daddy, I'd rather be *me* than anyone else in the world." She did not really understand what she was saying, but the very fact that she said it was significant. Many older people do not understand what they mean, either, when they suddenly catch on to the answer to the life question "Who am I?" For example, I was talking recently to a friend and asked her, suddenly, without warning, "Who are *you?*" She looked astonished, thought a moment, and then said: "I am a human being who is female, thirty-five years old, married, living in comfortable circumstances, works hard, enjoys life—"

"That's fine," I interrupted, "but I can find fifty women in the next two blocks who fit that description."

"What, then," she asked, "what makes *me* different?"

I answered: "The thing that makes you different from anyone else is that you are *you* and there is nobody else like you. This is it!"

"Well, that solves the identity problem as far as I am concerned," she declared. "I am *me,* and I am the only one like me. I *like* that!"

Clearly she had missed the point. Because she was looking for an easy, complete answer, she took the statement in the most superficial way. Actually, as I have said, the implications of the words "I am me" are quite complex. The expression involves a deep-seated awareness of the many facets of our personality. Why do we react as we do? How do we approach life and its meaning, our sense of values and our concept of our own state of being at a given time? Eventually my friend may come to an understanding of what she was so ready to accept, but it takes much thought to do this.

At the core of the answer to the question of identity lies the need for each of us to recognize our uniqueness. All of us have many things in common, but at the same time there is something in each of us that makes us different from anyone else. The resolution of the question of identity thus lies in this feeling of uniqueness, not a uniqueness that sets us apart but one that enables us to *participate,* to relate to others and make contributions that no one else in the world can. Each of us has a distinct attitude, approach, and value system, whether we realize it or not. It is true that we learned our value systems from others, but one reason so many people have difficulty in knowing who they are is that they have never bothered, or been able, to sort out and develop a value system of their own. Either they have taken the values of their parents and incorporated them into their own lives without any real comprehension of them, or they have rejected their parents' values without replacing them with something substantial.

Of course, none of us can reach a definitive point where we can say, *"This* is what I am, period." We constantly change; being is always becoming; we wear a variety of faces in our lives, from childhood through old age, but a person can have some very definite notions about himself—who he is—and when he does, his answer will not be in terms of the interpersonal world, his relations to other people. In other words, he will not answer in terms of his job or his relationship with others, in terms of his religion or his status in the community.

We cannot always judge when a person is well adjusted or happily married or secure in his own identity. Neither can we make judgments of the person who is obviously maladjusted. For example, you know someone who is a recluse. Instead of making fun or wondering why he is the way he is, you might teach yourself to think of him as a person with a poor sense of identity who has given up the search into which so many others have plunged headfirst. Beyond that, you probably must admit you know little. Since we obviously do not know ourselves very well, we rarely know what is going on inside others. We have to be careful not to take part-knowledge of another and try to develop it into an explanation of behavior that does not fit. We cannot ever expect to fully understand or judge others, because we cannot fully judge or understand ourselves. However, we can make educated guesses, and one way to do this is to observe the person who has apparently been able to organize his life constructively; he probably is well adjusted. I said *probably*, for there is no way of being certain.

People of every generation have been faced with problems of defining their own identity. The task has never been an easy one, but, as has been observed, it undoubtedly was not so difficult half a century ago as it is today. Someone said to me recently, "I wish I had grown up in my parents' generation. It was so easy then. You knew what was right and what was wrong. You knew how to make decisions. You knew who you were." While the older generations were not nearly so infallible as many people like to believe, I do think that sorting out our identities is more complex today than ever before—and it is going to become still more difficult in the future as we become more and more depersonalized by computers, machines, and still-to-be-invented contrivances that may take over more and more of our endeavors and skills.

How will we adjust as we travel farther and farther into space, making our world seem smaller every day? What will happen to us when television telephones are standard equipment in every home and office? Will our identity crises become greater as we pierce the sonic barrier in our everyday travels?

If we can bring ourselves to use diligence in working through each step in our lifetime series of identity crises, it is to be hoped that we can arrive at an acceptance of the fact that in a world of mass production, mass travel, mass communications, mass education, and mass population, there is one thing that is different from everything else—YOU. You are YOU and there is nobody else like you, and there never will be. That is your identity as it results from the effects of yesterday, as it expresses itself today, and as it constantly evolves all your life.

Different identity problems arise in different age groups. One group in which the problem is most acute is the young people entering the labor market. We find an increasing number who are unhappy because they feel they must begin at the bottom. Since their concept of themselves has never really been developed, they tend to attach their own sense of values to what they *do*. Many are well trained and highly skilled, and feel that to begin at the bottom in business would be a strike against them as persons. Unfortunately, their desire to start at the top is usually accompanied by a wish to begin at a high salary. By placing a dollar sign in front of their sense of identity, they seem to be saying that unless they begin their careers at a certain level they will feel worthless and thus lack a sense of their own being.

This sort of situation is compounded by still another manifestation of the identity crisis, the need everyone seems to have today to be in charge of something or someone. I seldom meet anyone anymore who is just a worker. Nearly everyone has a title. There are no more garbagemen, only sanitary engineers. The typewriter mechanic is a customer service engineer. The boss's girl Friday is an executive secretary. Titles give status; they also provide easy answers when one is asked who he is. They provide easy answers but not correct ones, for they explain not who one *is* but what he *does*.

In our success-oriented culture it is very important to be outstanding in one's job. Many people consider themselves failures as persons if they are failures in their work. One cannot help but suspect that a great many who fail in their work are motivated to fail, at least in part, by a desire to destroy themselves. In such people, failure in a job can be a form of suicide.

A salesman I know is this kind of person. At forty-six he has failed at everything he has ever undertaken. He has never really grown up. His marriage collapsed, and he has been fired from an endless succession of jobs. Rather than try to motivate him to do better work, I attempted to encourage him to develop a better regard for and knowledge of himself. Eventually I hope he will be able to approach a new job, determined to succeed rather than fail.

The question of self-destruction as related to identity—or the lack of it—should also be mentioned in connection with the race riots of the last several years in the Watts section of Los Angeles as well as in Newark, Detroit, and other cities, and in the rampages of frustration after the assassination of the Rev. Dr. Martin Luther King early in 1968. These outbursts were so complex that to isolate one element would be unfair. Yet the aspect involving the question of identity has not been emphasized enough. While the struggle for civil rights was an element in triggering the riots, in retrospect it must remain only one. I say this because "civil rights" is a constructive concept; the riots were wantonly self-destructive. If we look at the violence in terms of the identity crisis, we gain a better understanding of what happened.

Because of limitations placed upon them by society, and to a degree by themselves, residents of our American ghettos have not been able to develop a sense of personal identity. Though physically adults, many have not had the opportunity to develop an adult sense of being. They are confronted by many of the same emotional frustrations the small child faces when he begins to come to grips with the idea that he is a person in a world populated by other persons who are like him but also very different from him. Just as a child does not develop a sense of his own worth through a "handout" from his parents, so the people of the ghettos will not develop a sense of their own identity through the "handouts" of society—these can at best be only stopgap measures. The problems of the Negro will never be resolved unless a way is found to help him develop self-respect, i.e., identity as an individual after he achieves a sense of group identity.

The ghetto concept can be applied to another member of our society—Mom. She lives in a kind of ghetto, too, in which she has an identity problem of her own. Home is her ghetto. Women groping for their egos in bedroom, living room, and kitchen often find a panacea in childbearing. They act as though fertility makes them unique. One can only suspect that a woman so advertising her temporary self-importance did not feel like much of a person before she became pregnant. This is tragic, for almost any cow in a field can reproduce. At best, it is a rather tenuous way of getting a feeling of identity, and the women who achieve it thus are those you hear saying some years later, "I am only a housewife," or who find no purpose in life after their children have left home. The woman who says, "I am only a housewife," either has a weak identity or is trying to cut everyone else down in size; what she may be trying to say is that she feels she is more important—but she still does not know who she really is.

One woman who came to me for counseling always identified herself in terms of her relationships with others. If people catered to her she felt elated; if they ignored her or did not respond to her desire for attention, she felt rejected and dejected. Her sense of being existed only in her response to the actions of others as they related to her. Naturally her concept of herself was always in jeopardy. It has taken a long time for her to come to realize that other people often do and say what they do to deal with their own needs and problems, and that their treatment of her does not necessarily give any reflection of how worthwhile *she* is. By not being able to sort out the reactions of others in a more objective fashion, she makes herself more comfortable with herself.

The person who has some sense of identity is much freer to belong—really belong—than the one who is still floundering, for the simple reason that he is able to adjust to the moods of those around him and to develop a measure of objectivity. Some people do this by belonging in the popular sense of the word—by joining groups. Here again, however, we often encounter an identity problem. The chronic joiner may be frantically trying to find out who he is by belonging to as many organizations as he can. The man involved in Lions, Kiwanis,

Rotary, Optimist, and every other club you can think of is often regarded by his friends as gregarious, outgoing, and so on, but he may be the one who is looking hardest for his identity, while the quiet, retiring nonjoiner may have a much better notion of who he is.

In this vein we find the trophy collectors. I have a friend whose home is filled with accolades—to him. The house is almost a shrine—to *him*. He also finds it necessary to tell anyone who will listen how much money he makes, how much his car cost, the price of his wife's mink coat, ad nauseam. When he joins a club, he *must* become president. Well adjusted? I would think that he does not seem to have the slightest idea of his identity.

The crisis of belonging—or not belonging—is put into sharp focus in Ionesco's play *Rhinoceros,* in which all but one of the characters have such an intense need to belong, to be together, to be identified as a group, that they are willing to give up their individual identities to become rhinoceroses, to join the herd. An entire village—save the one man—become members of the herd. That man was not able to live as a man, but he could go out and die as one, knowing who he was.

There really is scarcely a group within our culture that has not been touched by the problem of identity, whether it be teen-agers, college students, young mothers, divorced couples, men and women in middle age, the old and senile, or the bereaved. Who are they? How can they find out who they are? Who are *you?* How can you find out who *you* are? All of us have many chances to try to resolve the question. Our answers depend on how we wear our various faces from childhood through old age, how we meet life's joys and sorrows, successes and failures. To help you in your search for your own answers, let us explore some of the problem areas, find out how some people have failed and others have found ways to cope with their own problems—and those of others.

2

"I Wanted to Be Somebody"

Robert Benjamin Smith, an eighteen-year-old Mesa, Arizona,
high school boy, put every parent, teacher, minister, counselor,
psychiatrist, and psychologist on trial the morning of Saturday,
November 12, 1966, when he walked into a beauty parlor and
shot seven women and children, killing five of them. He did
it, he said, to *"be somebody,"* and he laughed every time he
pulled the trigger.

Until that November day, Robert was a quiet, introspective
boy who kept to himself most of the time when he was not at
school. He stayed so close to home that the neighbors hardly
knew he existed. At school, he was polite but aloof. His outward maturity won him election to the student council, not
because he was popular but because the other students felt
they needed someone like him to serve. His marks were excellent in the subjects he liked and better than average in those
he took because he had to. "Uncommunicative but coopera-

tive" was the way he was described by his gym teacher, who was also his counselor. No one ever knew of Robert's dating a girl and he was friendly with none, although he was one of the best-looking boys in the school. He preferred to be alone with his books and his thoughts. What those thoughts were no one had an inkling until that explosive Saturday morning.

Robert lived with his parents and a younger sister in the small (population 50,000), largely Mormon city of Mesa, sixteen miles east of Phoenix. His father had retired as an Air Force major and had moved his family to Mesa, where he went to work for an electronics company. The family, regarded as pleasant but aloof, had lived in Mesa about a year when the outwardly uneventful life of Robert Benjamin Smith took a dramatic turn. It was Saturday, a day many schoolboys like to sleep late. But Robert had been planning for this day. He awakened at six-thirty, got out of bed, put on a blue and white pin-striped shirt, blue trousers, and canvas sneakers. He picked up a brown paper shopping bag he had methodically packed the night before and quietly left the house, walking toward the business section of the city.

The boy walked a mile and a half to the Rose-Mar College of Beauty, which was just opening when he arrived. He watched an employee enter and followed her in. Another employee arrived, and then three women who had appointments to have their hair set by student beauticians. One woman brought her two small daughters with her.

No one paid any attention to Robert until he drew a .22-caliber pistol from the paper bag and fired a shot into a mirror. The gun he used had been given to him by his parents for target practice three months earlier. On that day he began planning to kill as many people as he could.

The women and children were terrified as the boy ordered them into a back room, where he forced them to lie on the floor in a circle, with their bodies extending out like the spokes of a wheel. One of the beauticians warned the boy that at least forty people would be there shortly. His response was that he was "sorry" but he had not brought enough ammunition for them. Grinning, he walked around the circle, shooting each of his captives twice. He reloaded his pistol from the paper bag three times. The women and children lay there in terror as they were shot, one by one.

While he was still shooting, the manager of the school arrived, saw what was happening, and ran next door to call the police. Ambulances rushed the victims to a hospital, where five were pronounced dead. Two were wounded, a beautician and one of the little girls. The other child, aged three, had been stabbed after she was shot because, as Robert explained calmly later, "she kept jumping around."

Throughout the mass murder, Robert laughed. Apparently he never stopped laughing. Nor did he flee. He just stood silently by until the police came to take him away, and he willingly and unremorsefully confessed what he had done. "I shot some people," he told police. "They're back there. The gun is in that sack."

The policemen found the gun. The bag also contained the hunting knife Robert had used to stab the little girl, plastic sandwich bags, nylon rope, rubber gloves, ammunition, and a container of powder. His original plan had been to bind his victims, put the bags over their heads, tie pieces of rope around their necks, and watch them suffocate. He had bought the bags for this purpose, but he had miscalculated—they were too small to fit over a human head.

When Robert was taken to court for arraignment, he remained calm as he teetered back and forth in a high-backed chair. Occasionally, he smiled while waiting for his attorney to appear.

News of the terrible crime swept through Mesa and into the homes of the people who had known Robert. His teachers, classmates, and neighbors began remembering things about him, and the authorities started putting together bits and pieces of his life. Carl Heath, the Mesa high school basketball coach who was counselor to Robert, said the boy had been an excellent student and had never caused any trouble. "He was no mixer but there was never any evidence of hostility on his part toward others," Heath said. There were several unusual things about the lad, however. "After showering with the rest of the fellows after phys-ed class, Smith would usually be found sitting on the curb, looking over magazines or books— usually those having to do with science," the teacher recalled. And another thing: "It's funny—even after a year in the tumbling class, he couldn't do the simplest roll. After a year in softball, he couldn't bring the bat back far enough to make a decent swing. Just lack of coordination, I guess."

Robert's classmates remembered him as always wanting to be "known." Yet, as one recalled, "he was a loner even though he was a senior council representative. Nobody ever seemed to talk to him or walk around with him at school." A boy in his class said, "I'm sure he never dated a girl at our school."

Several students recalled that young Smith had been carrying a small hunting knife in a back pocket and when asked about it, shrugged off questions and refused to comment. Fellow students kidded him a lot about the detective stories he read, but he did not react to this. He participated in no activities and was regarded as "not the type for that." A "loner," he was considered "very intelligent and very nervous."

Other aspects of his personality were pieced together. A member of a special teacher-supervised seminar group for the brighter students, including Robert, said the boy once advocated using germ warfare to wipe out all Southeast Asians because "they're all animals and they're not important." The seminar teacher recalled that Robert often daydreamed and that once when she broke into his reverie with a question he seemed disturbed. Students said that he "did not value human life very much" and that in their discussions he ridiculed "love and compassion."

A student who described himself as Robert's best friend said that despite their closeness, he had never been in the boy's home. "He never talked about his family," the friend said. "I always met him on a corner somewhere."

Robert's classmates recalled further that he idolized the outlaw Jesse James and had a collection of pictures of Napoleon. In a classroom discussion, Robert once became "quite upset that Napoleon's march on Russia failed," one student said.

Mrs. Evelyn Denton, Robert's English teacher, said that he daydreamed in class and that his biggest disappointment in school had been her rejection of his suggestion that the school present *Harvey,* a play about an imaginary rabbit.

Neighbors along the neat block of modest houses where the

Smiths lived said they were "very quiet but wonderful people" who seldom associated with others. The boy was considered "very pleasant" but never was seen with anyone and appeared to be distant from his father. One neighbor said he had lived across the street from the Smiths for five months, unaware that Robert existed.

A stricken school counselor declared: "I saw the withdrawal in this boy, his lack of emotion. Yet, because he wasn't a disturbance or a troublemaker, I just didn't find the time to help him."

"Tell me what I should have known," said an anguished teacher. "I contend that as long as I live I would never pick Robert from my class as the one who would do something like this."

Newspapers began running interviews with psychiatrists and psychologists, several of whom agreed without seeing the boy that he was a schizophrenic who had inadequate relationships with women. "I would say it is not so much his problem of dating but . . . possibly a bad relationship with his mother and sister," said one. Another indicated a belief that the boy had sought recognition in this way, to become "someone" for a moment, which is what the boy himself had already said. "In any case," said a third, "if he had received psychiatric help, there is a good chance he would not have performed this act."

Meanwhile, the boy's family acted dramatically. As soon as Robert was arrested, a lawyer was retained—and a psychiatrist was called in to begin immediately to give "intensive psychiatric care and treatment" to Robert. The stunned parents issued a statement through the attorney saying: "Mr. and Mrs.

Robert L. Smith are extremely grief-stricken over the terrible tragedy wrought upon mankind by their disturbed boy. They extend their heartfelt sympathy to relatives and friends of the victims."

Then came what may be the most important statement of all, and one that explains the purpose in relating this story: "They are interested in conferring with authorities in the near future in an effort to help parents the world over detect such latent mental illness in a child, and thus, if possible, prevent any more of these insane homicides from occurring," the lawyer said.

(Subsequently Robert was found guilty of five counts of first-degree murder and two counts of assault with intent to commit murder. Under Arizona law, this meant that the boy would be sentenced to death in the gas chamber.)

What went wrong to turn an outwardly peaceable boy into a murderer? Why hadn't his family noticed anything was amiss? Or had they concluded Robert was "different" and simply shrugged it off? Aren't there many youngsters who are withdrawn and antisocial and yet grow up to be talented musicians, scientists, or writers? What were the gaps in the school's relationships with students that kept anyone from suspecting this was a deeply troubled boy who needed help? It is on these counts that Robert Smith has put those who had known him and, in a sense, all of society on trial.

The end of his ordeal marked only a beginning for his family. How are his parents going to face their own grief and guilt and the rest of the world, and how is the world going to regard the parents? What can be done to help and understand them as they try to cope with their misery?

This case is an extreme one, but there have been too many of these extremes in recent years, the most notable, of course, being that of Lee Harvey Oswald, who was found by a court psychiatrist to have schizophrenic symptoms when he was thirteen years old and who grew up to change the course of history by murdering a President of the United States. Although Oswald's identity problem was diagnosed, at least superficially, nothing was done about it. His mother brushed off the psychiatric report, and the court did not act further—and a monumental tragedy resulted.

In Robert's case, no one was even aware of his problem, it appears. Nor, apparently, was anyone aware of the deep-seated sickness of Leo Held, an outwardly quiet, retiring thirty-nine-year-old laboratory technician in a paper mill who killed six people and wounded six others in a shooting spree in Loganton, Pennsylvania, late in 1967. Held had appeared to be a quiet, peaceful citizen, devoted to his wife and children, and a member of the local school board and the board of directors of a Boy Scout troop. Immediately after the shootings, everyone expressed astonishment. Then they began thinking—and talking.

Held had been "blackballed" from his car pool because the other members considered him too fast a driver. He had seemed edgy in the days before the mass murders because he had been passed over for a promotion at the plant. He tended to pick arguments with his neighbors; once he accused a neighbor of encroaching on his property and another time he complained that smoke from neighbor's fires was drifting onto his lawn.

"He was not a good mixer," said W. Edward Meyer, president of the Loganton National Bank. "He was retiring almost to the point of being shy. But on the school board he'd take a firm stand and be obstinate and inflexible."

No one will ever know exactly what was going on inside Held to convert him from a Dr. Jekyll to a Mr. Hyde; he was so determined to elude capture by police that they had to shoot him to capture him, and he soon died of his wounds.

We can ask a number of questions, however. Where do the burdens of guilt in such cases really lie? Who was really to blame for Robert Smith, Leo Held, and Lee Harvey Oswald? Parents? Schools? Church? Social agencies? Who? What happened in the lives of these men that forced them to express their identities in such bizarre and destructive ways? Why couldn't they have developed a sense of worth that could have been expressed constructively? Could they have been helped, and if so, by whom?

In asking this last question, we also can properly inquire: At what point could the school, the church, the community, or the family have dealt with these identity crises? How and when does one go about helping anyone with a problem? Who should help?

Certainly, most troubled individuals do not act drastically or dramatically. However, damage is done, mainly to themselves, their families, and their immediate circle. Society always suffers a little with any degree of maladjustment. The tragedy begins mainly in the family, where many experiences occur as a result of family emotional problems but are neither adequately understood nor properly accepted by the family or others.

As a pastoral counselor and psychotherapist I see a good

many people, young and old, who *are* aware they have problems, and whose families are often also aware. There is no way of measuring the tragedies that have been averted by counseling and psychotherapy, but those of us who work in this field are convinced that many have been helped to learn to deal with their own problems and the problems of others, and to function more adequately in relation to society. Pastoral counseling is a relatively new specialty within the ministry. A number of clergymen of all faiths have received intensive psychological training and clinical experience, and a number of us have gone through in-depth analysis ourselves in the course of becoming accomplished in the techniques of psychotherapy. The specialty has arisen because increasing numbers of distressed individuals have been taking their problems to ministers rather than to doctors, psychologists, or psychiatrists. There is a shortage of psychiatrists and other social scientists who counsel, and so pastoral counselors are making themselves increasingly available to try to help the less anxious and disturbed people deal with their problems. Pastoral counselors work in close partnership with psychiatrists, psychologists, and other professionals, seeking their counsel whenever it is necessary.

When I was on the staff of a mental health clinic in New York, I worked with a teen-age boy who might conceivably have become destructive if he had not received help. Whether he would have taken such drastic steps as Robert Smith it is impossible to say, but his case does offer an example of what can be done and what, in fact, is being done all over the country.

The boy—we will call him Joe—was much like Robert

Smith, quiet and withdrawn. Instead of having a father, even one with whom he had been unable to be close, as appeared to be the case with the Smith boy, Joe's father had died when he was very small, and he had a stepfather he resented. Joe began getting in trouble in school when he was in the eighth grade. He became surly toward his mother, stopped studying, and finally was suspended for shoving a teacher.

At this point, his mother consulted her minister, who referred the boy to me. He kept his first appointment reluctantly and was not very communicative. A slight, sandy-haired boy, he slumped into a chair with an expression that seemed to dare me to get him to talk. When I indicated an impression that he had acted violently toward his teacher, his attitude changed. One of the first things I learned from Joe was that he had not intended the incident with the teacher as an expression of violence. He maintained that he rather liked the teacher and had shoved him in what he considered a playful manner.

The teacher obviously did not interpret it that way, and it took me weeks to convince Joe of this. His inability to differentiate between acceptable and unacceptable social behavior was a stumbling block for a long time, but he finally came to understand that it is not appropriate for a student to shove a teacher, even in fun.

When Joe first came to see me, it was clear that he had never developed any real identification of himself; he had built a barrier of resentment and anger around himself. He did not like himself very much, so he did not particularly care for anyone else either. He resented the presence of his stepfather. Temporarily, at least, he found the father figure he needed in me, and it was through his being able to relate to me that he began to learn how to become a man. We got along well after a few rugged sessions, but only after I was able to set certain limits for him, limits that at an earlier time should have been set by his parents. I assisted him in realizing that his acting-out helped no one. "It is all right if you become angry at your teacher," I told him, "but do not lose your temper and do not show it with any physical action. Don't do anything that will get you into trouble."

Then I helped him understand that, whether he liked them or not, there were certain things, such as performing household chores assigned him by his mother, that it was appropriate and advantageous for him to do. The most difficult point on which I found it necessary to get Joe to cooperate involved obeying rules set at home, whether they were right or wrong. "If your mother or stepfather tells you to do something or forbids you to do something, sometimes you must accept their rulings," I said. More than once, I must admit, I agreed with Joe that they were wrong, but I also was able to impress upon him the need to learn to abide by rules that made sense even if he wished to do otherwise.

After a time, Joe began to warm to our relationship and brought me a small gift—a ballpoint pen. My genuine pleasure at this acceptance had gratifying results. Joe had started to respect me as a person, and this was an outgrowth of his ability, at last, to respect himself. More important, he began to understand that the demands made on him in school and at home, which he had regarded as excessive, were not as far beyond his capabilities as he had thought.

The most difficult aspect of the therapy was that Joe was extremely resentful of his own father—even angry with him—for having died. His relationship with me became an acceptable temporary substitute. He began imitating little things I did—gestures, use of words, and so on. Once after I had told him about having been on a fishing trip, he returned for his next session filled with lore about fishing. It was obvious he had paid a special visit to the public library for his research. He became interested in my wife and children and symbolically became another "son."

Gradually Joe began to emerge from his isolation. He went out and made friends and did things in which he was interested. Instead of standing on a street corner and watching other youngsters at play, he would join in. He developed a hobby of building model airplanes and found other boys who were interested in the same thing. It was quite a day when he came in and told me that he had asked a girl for a date for the first time—and she had accepted.

Joe had many of the characteristics of Robert Smith, but he was lucky, because his mother saw that something was wrong and acted—in time.

There are many boys—and girls—like Joe in the world, and there are countless other people, adults and children, with different kinds of problems. These are mainly people who are not actually mentally ill or in need of institutional care. But, while they may not deteriorate into Robert Smiths or Leo Helds or Lee Harvey Oswalds, they have problems that are becoming too much for them and so they have become disrupting influences in the home, in the office, in school, or wherever they may be. What we must consider is what you and I can do about it. Should we do anything, and if so, when? The Bible suggests we are our brother's keeper. Are we really? And if we are, what does this mean and how does it relate to dealing with the emotional conflicts of those around us?

3

What's the Matter with Jimmy?

"I don't know what is the matter with Jimmy. He refuses to
do his homework and I know he is never going to get into college. His father and I can't do a thing with him."

"If you think *you* have a problem, you should see Priscilla.
She monopolizes the telephone with inane chatter. She picks
on the younger children. She won't help with the dishes or
housework, not even for her allowance. Her hi-fi set is driving
us out of our minds."

"Well, our difficulty with Jane is that she won't clean her
room. It's a mess. All she does is play phonograph records and
primp for the boys. We can't get her to wear decent-looking
clothes either. She is a sight."

"What do you do with a boy who has let his hair grow down
to his shoulders and wants to quit school to earn money for a
car? I'm about at the end of my rope."

"Harry hasn't said a polite word to his father in weeks. He

spends all his time in his room looking at pictures in *Playboy* magazine."

On and on it goes. You hear parents of teen-agers talking this way at lunch, over bridge or cocktails, on the golf course, at dinner parties—wherever one encounters parents of teen-agers. The talk is monopolized by "What's the matter with Jimmy? We can't do a thing with him," etc.

Of course, we do hear about what is "right" about our young people, but often this comes in the form of parental bragging about a youngster who has just won a National Merit Scholarship, been accepted by Harvard, or built a rocket in the cellar. Parents who report such feats often tend to make it appear as though *they* had been responsible for the accomplishments. They are involved in a rat-race for status, and part of their status comes from having youngsters who are rated as achievers. This is another way of saying that some parents get at least some of their own identity from the accomplishments of their children. In the course of the competition forced upon him, the average teen-ager is placed in a kind of limbo, while the youngster with problems is pressured and criticized and the bright one is extolled, often out of proportion to his achievements.

Indeed, since teen-agers are now the largest population group in our country, with the result that we have a comparably vast number of parents of teen-agers, conversations about youngsters sometimes go on and on to a point where the complaints seem endless.

A teen-ager refuses to take a bath or comb his hair. He talks back to his father, giving the impression that to his way of thinking anyone over twenty is bordering on idiocy. He sulks when he does not get his way. He loses his temper easily. He lies. He daydreams a lot, mainly about how to get rich quick without doing any work. When it comes to a serious discussion about his future, he shrugs and slouches out of the room with a sigh that sounds like the air being let out of a tire.

The pouting, back-talking, recalcitrant girls are with us, too. Sometimes boys and girls engage in petty thefts from dime stores or snap off hub caps or antennas from automobiles. They may commit a minor act of vandalism, such as breaking a window in the home of "that crab who lives down the street" or uprooting her tenderly nurtured bulbs.

All of this becomes a trial and tribulation for parents, many of whom think it is happening only in *their* families—until they start comparing notes with others. They discover that it is the kind of behavior that tends to occur some time after the ages of ten or eleven, and often later, when a child is going through a period of rapid physical growth and painful psychological adjustment that can be one of the most traumatic experiences of his life.

The child in adolescence is often puzzled about who he is or where he really belongs. His parents confuse him by expecting all sorts of things of him that he is not yet really able to comprehend. He suffers from fears spawned by awakening sexual desires and an ambivalence between dependency and independence. It is time for him to develop his own value system, and he needs help as he gropes into his future. But too often he does not get the assistance he longs for. The high rate of unwed teen-age parents is attributable, at least in part, to the existence of this moral void. Young people get the idea they are supposed to be sophisticated, i.e., adult, in their behavior, but they are often not psychologically equipped for it.

In addition to the stresses of physical development, the child entering his teens is also confronted by social pressures. Dating becomes important, if not to him, to his mother and father—particularly his mother. He is encouraged to participate in sports and to be the star of the football team. And he is expected to earn the highest grades in his class and get into the best college, and, while he is at it, receive a lucrative scholarship to ease the drain on the family bank account. The high and rising suicide rate among young people is one result of these pressures, and this we will discuss in detail later.

Indeed, the teen-ager is expected to go through an almost unbelievable series of experiences, some of which are:

• Adjusting to the physical changes that occur in puberty, learning to use his body as an adult, and coming to accept himself as he is physically.

• Learning to understand the sort of behavior that is expected of him if he is to be a socially responsible and constructive citizen.

• Separating himself emotionally from his parents in preparation for the day when he parts physically from them.

• Choosing a vocation and developing talents and skills he needs to work as a useful member of society and as a self-supporting individual.

• Preparing for the demands and responsibilities of marriage and parenthood.

To a certain extent the way in which a teen-ager works through and solves—and even survives—the problems of adolescence depends on his early development and his first human relationships, at home and later at school. The ability of a parent to show genuine love and respect for a child from the day he is born and to supply the needs that generally make him satisfied and contented is reflected when a child comes to adolescence. Rigid parents, for example, sometimes feel they must teach a child a "lesson" before he is able to accept responsibility. One common area in which overanxious parents pressure a child comes very early in life—toilet training. If a parent enforces rigid requirements in this procedure, a child may well enter adolescence feeling that life already has made demands on him that he cannot meet. His feeling of frustration is heightened by the changes he goes through in adolescence, and he may find himself eventually thrust into a frenzied world where he is unable to do anything without feeling that he is under pressure to act in another way.

In an ideal situation, a balance is struck so that a child who is allowed freedom does not as a consequence act like a wild animal. Limits must be set, of course. A child needs rules and regulations, boundaries within which he can be himself. Unfortunately, we find many markedly immature adults who come for counseling suffering from the failure of their parents to set reasonable limits for them when they were growing up. To use an extreme example, while there is no objection to a child's riding in a car or sitting in a make-believe auto and pretending he is in the driver's seat, he must be made to understand that he cannot actually drive the vehicle.

In communicating rules and regulations, the reasons for them obviously should be made clear. This gives a child a greater feeling of security. When he says, "Why can't I do it?"

it is a mistake to limit the response to a mere "because" or "You're too young to understand." He *must* have a reason.

The quest for freedom and identity is bound to cause some misbehavior in early adolescence, but this is not necessarily a foreboding of trouble later. A youngster may simply be trying out a certain amount of freedom to see if he can get away with it. He may merely be beginning to draw away from home. This period of testing is one in which parents can review their own attitudes toward their child, for it is a time when a youngster may be "acting out" (letting off steam is the old-fashioned term) as a result of too much parental control. In treatment, we often find it necessary to help a patient soothe his own conscience because he still feels overly guilty about some of his own childhood infractions, which occurred when his parents, out of their own feelings of insecurity, were afraid to deal with his mistakes.

Generally, the more secure parents are, the more secure their children will be, and security comes from a sound sense of identity. One would think it would not be necessary to point this out, but I have seen several people who as adults still were suffering from their parents' lack of security. One who comes to mind is an eighteen-year-old girl who called on me for help. Her father was a successful professional man, but he still felt insecure as a result of an impoverished youth in Eastern Europe. His insecurity made him dogmatic, judgmental, and quite certain in his own mind that he was the final authority on any matter that confronted his family.

The girl—Rose, we will call her—tended to be vivacious and receptive to new ideas. She leaned toward artistic and unorthodox attire—black stockings, gaudy dangling earrings, white lipstick, etc. Although she was far from a beatnik or hippie, she bordered on being slovenly at times; it was part of her rebellion against her father. In these and other ways she was quite unlike her father, and she was torn between the way she wanted to live and the way he wanted her to be. This brought about not only rebellion but a terrible guilt about her rebellion. It also created in her an ambivalence toward her parents and toward other aspects of her life. She had trouble studying. She was unable to concentrate. She could not make up her mind about working, dating, and friends.

This was reflected in her relations with everyone she encountered. She came to feel that people would be hurt if she did not give in to them, if she stood up and told them what she really thought, if she turned down a date with a boy she did not like. All of these reactions were projections of her own fear that she would not be able to cope with life if anyone treated her the way she wanted to treat others.

For a long time, Rose was unable to see her own deep dependency needs because she concealed them in a concern for others' feelings. Over a period of months she managed to tell me about it. The more she talked, the more she came to see that she was the victim of well-meaning but difficult parents. Eventually, without consulting anyone, she went out and got a job in an office and rented her own apartment. Later she enrolled in night school. She came to realize at last that she was a person in her own right and that there was nothing wrong with that.

Much of the misery encountered in her late teens stemmed from what happened to her during her eleventh year, when her parents were appalled to discover suddenly that their child no longer looked to them for rules of behavior. Rather, she, like others her age, sought the approbation of her contemporaries. At this time, a parent who regards a child as his *possession* is likely to encounter a great deal of trouble and possibly even heartbreak. To a degree, beginning at this age and for the rest of his adolescence, a child who feels adequately loved and respected will act as though he is not afraid of his parents or of disobeying them. Within limits, he will be able to test the world outside his home and, as a result, he may get into minor scrapes that annoy his parents. As long as these episodes are not too frequent, destructive, or antisocial, parents should not be alarmed about them.

It is at this age that children start thinking their parents are not quite bright. This is only natural, for if a child can convince himself that his mother and father are stupid, it becomes easier to separate himself from them. Very young children regard their parents as perfect, but later, youngsters need a justification in their own minds for casting off their feelings of dependency. Coming to regard parents as stupid, old-fashioned, or whatever becomes adequate justification for cutting the proverbial silver cord. Each succeeding generation has to feel that it is more rebellious than any other—and parents also tend to regard their children as worse rebels than *they* were.

A family I knew some years ago dealt with the matter of rebellion in an intelligent way. There were five normally rambunctious and unusually bright children in this household. One Halloween they decided to "get even" with a cranky old lady who lived in their block. They had a number of grievances against her, principally that she had failed to pay them for shoveling snow off her walk the previous winter. So they rang her doorbell on Halloween and pelted her wallpaper with eggs and tomatoes. She recognized the children, who had made no attempt to hide their identities, and immediately complained to their parents. The father volunteered to pay for new wallpaper and informed the youngsters that they would have to earn the money.

The youngsters thought their father had taken a pretty old-fashioned approach, but what they did not know was that he had found it very difficult to be severe with them about their vandalism. If truth were told, he recalled even worse pranks he had been involved in when he was their age, but he managed to make his point in this cultural game and let the children go on believing they had been much more mischievous than he would ever have thought of being at their age. If he had not taken this attitude, he would have been doing the children a disservice, for they had gone beyond the limits of acceptable social behavior and had to be so informed—firmly and at once.

Some parents are afraid of their children under circumstances such as these—and show it. This can cause trouble. To let a child know you are afraid of him makes him both insecure and unsure of his identity. As we have indicated, there is a delicate balance to be struck between permitting a youngster to have the freedom he needs and creating an atmosphere in which he feels safe, secure, and able to learn what he can and cannot do. The child who is made to feel guilty about his actions and attitudes often becomes too aggressive. The late Dr. William Menninger once said that "the kind of behavior that leads to guilt feelings is called aggression; it is an expression of hostility."

The biological aspects of adolescence also cannot be over-emphasized. This is the time when girls reach menarche and find themselves on the threshold of their childbearing years. Boys' voices deepen, hair begins to appear on parts of their bodies, and there is a stirring of sexual feelings. Teen-agers find themselves with the bodies of adults and the emotions of children, and the conflict can be bewildering.

If you stop to think back to your own adolescence, you may be able to understand that even a child of a later generation, no matter how sophisticated or how well prepared he is for these changes, can experience them with feelings of anxiety and even fear. It is amazing to find as many young people as we do who have had little or no orientation to the physical changes that occur in adolescence. Parents can do a great deal to provide enough understanding to cushion youngsters in the shock period known as growing up. In this era of frankness, it should not be necessary to remind a mother of her obliga-tion to inform her daughter of what will take place and why, and how to prepare for it. Boys, too, need to be alerted to the increasing activity of their sex glands so they can understand why they have desires, erections, and nocturnal emissions. Ig-norance about these things can produce terror and confusion and possibly even tragedy.

Some years ago, one of the most shocking murders of a generation was committed in Chicago by a teen-age boy who had gone through puberty at the age of eight or nine with-out his parents' being aware of it and without having any idea himself of what was taking place. This plunged him into a series of sex crimes. That boy was William Heirens, whose crimes became progressively worse until he kidnaped, murdered, and dismembered a little girl he found sleeping in a crib. All of this was done in an unconscious attempt at sexual gratification. Heirens was committed to an institution for life, despite the pleas of his mother to the judge to let him go because she was certain that he was really a good boy and would never get into trouble again. The bewildered, grieving mother simply did not understand what had happened.

I never cease to be amazed at the number of women seeking counseling who grew up with little or no education about bodily functions or venereal disease. Boys are often even more ill-prepared, it seems to me. Curiosity about sex is natural during early adolescence. While masturbation often occurs in infancy and early childhood, adolescence is the time when many youngsters, particularly boys, begin masturbating consciously. The attitude toward masturbation is much more enlightened today than it used to be, when all sorts of superstitions abounded about "man's secret sin," including the notion that it caused insanity or sterility. Only the most backward and uninformed parents still consider it either a sin or physically debilitating. Apart from release of built-up sexual tensions, masturbation can be explained this way: the adolescent finds himself between two worlds and he is not sure in which direction he wants to go. When the adult world becomes too frightening, he looks longingly back to the more comfortable and carefree world of the child. Sometimes he feels the need to return to a place where he feels comfortable, and in part, masturbation fulfills this need. Dr. Menninger subscribed to this theory, saying that "masturbation in adolescence is a way of slipping back to childhood where one is particularly interested in himself."

It is of utmost importance for parents to understand sexual development and to accept it as natural and normal and assume an enlightened attitude toward discussions of it.

Sometimes sex is involved in one of several danger signals parents can be alert for in rearing children, particularly adolescents. The ability to recognize these danger signs can help considerably in understanding children's problems, in learning to live with them, and in helping children themselves to deal with them. It also can make life easier for parents. Here are some of the red flags of adolescence:

1. *Exaggerated attitudes toward sex*

A youngster may think about sex and yet be afraid to discuss it with his parents. Many children will never talk about the subject with adults, preferring to exchange information—and misinformation—with other teen-agers. We all know of cases in which misguided or unguided youngsters have developed too great an interest in the opposite sex at too young an age, or too much interest in the same sex.

Of course, all young people do not develop along the same lines sexually or give evidence of interest in sex at a given time in their lives. Some are slower than others to awaken sexually. The alert and observant parent will watch for effeminate gestures or appearance in their teen-age sons and a tendency toward masculinity on the part of girls. This is not to say that an athletic girl or an artistic boy is going to grow up to be a homosexual, or that the long-hair styles favored lately by boys and the short haircuts girls are wearing signify sexual deviation, but when certain tendencies are overdeveloped or caricatured, the wise parent will try to communicate with his child about sex on a frank basis. If this is not possible, perhaps outside counseling should be sought.

2. *Antisocial "acting-out"*

It is normal for an average, developing teen-ager to rebel against parental control. This rebellion is a sign of his ambivalence between wanting to be a child who is taken care of and yearning to be an adult who is independent. Minor or mild acting-out in moderately antisocial ways need not be cause for alarm. Taking a hub cap or removing an apple from the corner fruit stand should not be considered a major infraction—unless it becomes a regular occurrence. At the same time, it should not be ignored, but rather should be dealt with in a gentle fashion.

More serious antisocial acting-out such as gang activity, including stealing, vandalism, and violence that results in juvenile delinquency is obviously a sign that something is deeply wrong.

3. *Wanton destructiveness*

A danger signal flashes unmistakably when a child or adolescent destroys his own property or that of others for no apparent reason. Also cause for alarm is a teen-ager who likes to inflict physical pain. Occasionally we encounter a child who takes pleasure in killing or torturing animals. Such a youngster needs immediate professional attention.

4. *Daydreaming*

It is perfectly acceptable for teen-agers to engage in daydreaming, and most of them apparently do. But healthy youngsters are able to emerge from their daydreams in order to do their school work, participate in extracurricular activities, and begin planning what they want to do with their lives. The inability to concentrate is another characteristic of teen-agers. It is not serious, as long as it does not happen all the time.

If inability to concentrate or persistent daydreaming inhibits a young person's ability to complete anything—studies, hobbies, games, etc.—then there may be trouble ahead. It is as teen-agers that professional baseball players often sign contracts and that the Army drafts boys and expects them to do their jobs. Girls begin training for nursing and teaching as teen-agers. In all of these activities it is necessary for young people to know how to focus their attention long enough to get their work done. If they can't, they may be in trouble.

5. *Extreme withdrawal*

Changes in mood are normal. One moment, hour, or day a youngster may be enthusiastic about being with the crowd, and in the next he may want to be alone. This is true of many adults, too. Adolescents often have violent shifts of mood and periods of deep depression. These need not be cause for parental despair, but there can come a time when withdrawal symptoms are marked and require professional attention. If a young person sulks for long periods, locks himself in, literally and figuratively, and has no friends; if he wants to be alone much of the time and does not do anything, there is reason for concern.

Some youngsters are more inner-directed and self-reliant than others, and all do not have the same degree of social development or the same needs for socialization. The teen-ager who is more interested in doing things by himself certainly is not necessarily sick; some of our great geniuses have been lifelong loners. But even the child who enjoys solitude should be encouraged gently to make friends and develop relationships outside the home.

6. *Lying*

This can be a danger signal. Sometimes parents make a federal case out of a lie told by a teen-ager even though it involves a matter of little or no consequence. This can create a problem where none really exists, for the youngster may be so irritated by his parents' overreaction that he continues telling lies—bigger and bigger ones—in rebellion. For example, a parent asks, "Did you take a bath?" The child says "Yes," when he has not. He says he did because he wants to go out and play ball and knows that if he says "No," his parents will confine him to the house. If he lied about this repeatedly for six months, then there would be cause for concern. But if a youngster lies once about a small matter such as a bath, it is sometimes best not to say anything. It may be more appropriate to ask him, "Why did you tell me you took a bath when you didn't?" If he feels free enough, he will tell you why. Then, if communication between parent and child is good, the parent can explain that lying is not the best way out. He might suggest that it would have been appropriate to say, "I didn't take a bath because I would have been late for the game."

When serious lying becomes evident, it is past time for seeking help for your teen-ager. An example of such an infraction is a statement by an adolescent, falsely charging a person with a crime. This sometimes happens and is a symptom of serious trouble.

7. *Violent moods*

As long as it is not destructive, anger is a normal human reaction, but rage can be serious. Destructive impulses can be a sign that an adolescent is unable to handle some of his deeper unconscious needs and desires.

There are danger signals a parent can look for in himself, too, including:

1. *A realization that there is no point of communication between his child and himself*

There should be times when a parent feels that he and his child are communicating on or near the same level. While a teen-ager is involved in developing his own system of values, he still needs to draw on the guidance of a mature person, which should be one or both of his parents. If there is no communication, he may find it difficult to establish a base upon which to build.

Exactly what is a value system? It is an internal organizational code that guides the way a person will act and react in life situations and experiences. It is the basis for ethical decisions and provides the foundation upon which interpersonal relationships in later life are developed. For example, in a home that stresses the acquisition of wealth as being of utmost importance, a child may develop a value system in which money is at the top of the hierarchy. If this is the case, he may decide that making money will produce the greatest "good" in his life, and everything he does will be pointed in this direction. Other aspects, such as social relationships, family life, the concept of fair play, etc., will rank after the desire to make money.

This also is the area in which a young person learns the basis for answering the questions "What should I do?" "Is what I am about to do right or wrong?" etc., in any given situation.

2. *A lack of mutual respect*

Implicit in the concept of communication between parents and children is a feeling of respect and regard for one another. Parents are often insistent that children respect them, but without acknowledging that respect also should flow the other way.

George is a good example of this. He came for counseling at the behest of his parents. At fifteen, he was regarded by them as disrespectful. He also had trouble with his studies and did not get along well with other youngsters. His father was well-meaning but at the same time an insecure martinet.

"I want George to show more respect for me and his mother," the father told me.

When I discussed the situation with George, he said he would not mind showing respect for his parents if they would treat him with a little consideration, too. I told George that two wrongs could never make a right, but admitted that he had a valid argument. The lines of communication between parents and children can be kept open only if there is mutual respect, and that includes respect for the rights of a teen-ager.

In George's case, I persuaded him to be more considerate of his parents and to treat them courteously. I also had several talks with the parents and suggested that they give him the same kind of treatment and have respect for his point of view, his privacy, and his tastes in music and clothes. It had never dawned on them that George had a right to be respected, too.

I did not have too difficult a time convincing them that an adolescent has as much right to privacy as do his parents. I told them that this right had to be determined in the context of the total family situation, of course, but that it existed nonetheless. "George also has a right to make his own decisions within certain limits," I said. "There are things concerning him that George has a right to decide. Of course, any of us must sometimes make a compromise with society if we are to live in it. And these compromises are dictated in part, at least, by propriety and good taste. But one also has a right to be himself."

3. Exploitation of children

Children have a distinct right not to be exploited. Many parents give their teen-agers weekly allowances with the proviso that certain rules must be followed or the money will be cut off. A young man we will call Jack had this problem. His father gave him two dollars a week for spending money during the school year. The boy was told that he would be expected to perform certain household chores but that there was no connection between this assignment and his allowance.

Two weeks later, his father asked him to wash the car. Jack had made a previous date with a friend for the appointed hour on Saturday morning, so he did not carry out his father's request. It had been customary for the father to give Jack his allowance each Saturday night, but on this evening he announced he was deducting fifty cents because Jack had not washed the car. Since that kind of condition had not been made clear at the outset, Jack was understandably angry. He rightly felt that his father was exploiting him. Parents should make agreements as explicitly as possible. That does not mean a youngster has to like the agreement, but it does mean that he has to know what it is.

4. Failure to carry out threats

A teen-ager also has certain rights because he is unable to provide for himself. These are the rights to shelter, food, and protection. I was appalled not long ago when a father said he felt he had a right to drastically curtail the amount of food his son was given to eat because the boy was not earning any money and also because he did not like some of the things the boy was doing.

Furthermore, the father said that if the boy did not "shape up" he would throw him out of the house. Since the youth was underage, I reminded the father that he would be violating a moral obligation and probably the law as well.

"You just can't do that," I told him.

"Well, when it comes down to cases, I probably wouldn't," he replied.

I then reminded him of the dangers a parent risks when he makes a threat to a teen-ager—or a child of any age, for that matter—that he either has no intention of carrying out or that even his own common sense will tell him he would not think of carrying out. Threatening to cut off food supplies or to evict a child falls into this category. These and lesser threats, when not carried out, undermine parental authority over a child and reduce the child's respect for *all* authority.

Naturally there is more to growing up and discovering one's identity than can be covered here. All we hope to do is to make parents and children aware of the great part the adolescent years play in developing a concept of self. Neither parents nor children should take their responsibilities lightly. This is the time when the young person is torn between the desire to become a person in his own right and to remain a child under the protection of Mother and Dad. The parent has an obligation to assist him as much as possible in this struggle. In rearing children, too many parents *insist* on their way rather than *assisting,* and that is one reason for the runaways, the hippies, and the breakdowns and suicides among teen-agers.

4

Give Your Kids a Chance

The car pulled into the black-topped driveway shortly after
midnight, as it had on many such Saturday evenings. The
ruddy-faced man behind the wheel paused to let his wife get
out and go into the house while he pulled into the garage. As
the trim, fortyish suburban housewife started to turn her front-
door key in the lock, she heard an unearthly cry.

"My God! Oh, my God!" her husband shouted. She ran to
investigate, let out a piercing scream, and fainted.

Dangling from a garage rafter in the full glare of the automobile headlights was the inert form of their eighteen-year-old
son, clad in dungarees and T-shirt. He had come home from
college unannounced and had hanged himself with a length of
clothesline while they were at their weekly bridge party.

The father frantically cut down the body and tried to revive
the boy with mouth-to-mouth resuscitation. A neighbor who
had heard the parents' cries rushed to the scene and then telephoned for an ambulance.

By that time the entire neighborhood had been aroused by the commotion, and the now conscious and distraught mother had been taken into the home next door.

An ambulance arrived, but the attendants could do nothing.

"Your boy is dead," a young doctor told the father.

"Why?" the father sobbed. "Why did he do it?"

Inside the house, resting on a tear-soaked pillow, was a note that gave part of the boy's answer.

"I can't stand being a failure," the boy had scrawled. "Forgive me for disappointing you."

A failure? At eighteen? Forgive what?

In the boy's own mind he was a failure because he had not been able to make the grade at an Ivy League college during a freshman year of struggling night and day to make acceptable marks. He had not wanted to go to that school. In fact, he had not wanted to go to college at all. It had been his dream to study art, but *his* desires had not coincided with what his parents thought was best for him, which meant they wanted him to be *somebody,* and being somebody meant getting a degree from a prestige school and then going into business and making a lot of money. He, like many a runaway and hippie, had been subjected to unbearable parental pressures. Instead of running away and losing himself in the teen-age "underworld," he had worked himself to the point of exhaustion trying to live up to their expectations. Now he was dead.

Whose failure was he? His parents'. Whose turn was it now to seek forgiveness? His guilt-ridden parents—too late.

This boy's suicide was not an isolated case. We all have read about juvenile suicides in the newspapers. About 1,000 American college students kill themselves every year, and about 90,000 others actively threaten suicide. Many of the youngsters who have destroyed themselves, or who have fallen into mental and emotional abysses, are victims of a social malignancy, the rat race of competition fomented by parents who use their children to compete with other parents in an effort to make up for their own disappointments and shortcomings. In other words, these parents are trying to foist tailormade identities on their children.

Pressures on youngsters today are monumental, as we have already seen, and often they become unbearable. True, suicide is an extreme that can and often does involve mental derangement at the moment of self-destruction, but we cannot overlook the conditions that produce that emotional state. Added to the suicides are the rising number of breakdowns of youngsters who cannot stand up to the brutal competition at school and the nagging at home with which they are confronted almost from the day they pick up their first kindergarten toys. Instead of enjoying carefree childhoods, they find themselves clawing their way through the years until they are adults, often bitter, frustrated, and faced with what they have been led to believe is failure because they do not measure up to parental hopes and specifications as to what and who they should be. And so they become dropouts—from school, from the family, and from society. Worse still, they are dropouts from themselves; they never have had a chance to even try to find out on their own who they are.

The stigma of being a dropout is too much for many youngsters who have lived their short lives branded as underachievers by often-overaspiring parents. The term "underachiever" carries with it a kind of social implication that is less than complimentary. Many of those so branded really are average kids whose needs for training, whose interests, and whose educational requirements cannot be met by a society that has made a demanding stereotype of success.

The status of going to college—the "right" college—becomes the most important thing in the lives of parents, with the result that, as in the case of the boy who killed himself, a youngster is forced to get out of his own league. The boy suicide might have done well in a smaller, less competitive school with a good art course and thus become adjusted to the idea of getting a college education. But his parents expected too much of him, instead of accepting what he wanted to do and realistically appraising his capabilities, as did one mother I know who confided in me: "My husband is disappointed because our boy is going to a 'minor league' school, but he has always thought our youngster was much smarter than he is. Actually, he is an average, delightful human being, and I, for one, am glad he chose a school where he is likely to succeed and have some fun doing it. He really has found himself."

We hear a lot about dropouts, particularly from high school but also from college. Actually, the rate of dropouts from high school is overemphasized because a larger percentage of our population is graduating from high school than ever before. Official government figures show that in the 1869–70 school year, there were 815,000 youngsters seventeen years old in our country. Of this number, 2 percent, or 16,000, were graduated from high school. By 1943–44 there were 2,410,000 young people in the seventeen-year-old age group, of whom more than 1,000,000 or 42.3 percent had received high school diplomas. Twenty years later, 76.7 percent or 2,302,000 of the nation's 3,001,000 seventeen-year-olds graduated. Unfortunately, the diminishing percentage of dropouts, who get an extravagant amount of publicity, are in too many instances headed for delinquency and therefore are a cause for public concern.

Another reason for concern is the fact that, while our teenage population is increasing rapidly, the number of available jobs is diminishing, with the result that efforts are being made to keep young people out of the labor market as long as possible. This is one of the reasons many more youngsters are going to college and then on to graduate school. Some economists have gone so far as to state that it might eventually be necessary to keep them dependent and studying until their late twenties.

Advanced schooling, at least in colleges and universities, is not what many young people need or want, however. Somewhere around 50 percent of all who enter college drop out before graduation; the attrition in the freshman classes is about 40 percent. This certainly raises a question whether these dropouts should have "dropped-in" at all.

The kinds of pressures that put this 40 percent in college were discussed in a recent "Dialogue on Adolescence" sponsored by the Children's Bureau of the Department of Health, Education and Welfare. Experts representing a broad spectrum of the populace dwelt at length on the uneasy plight of our young. Among them was Dr. Alfred J. Kahn, professor of social work at the Columbia University School of Social Work, who aptly summarized the pressures on young people in a kind of "shorthand terminology" he had developed.

First, he said, in an affluent suburbia "the most common adjustment pattern" can be labeled the *"rat-race"* subculture. "That is," he explained, "the kids' lives are dominated by the need to get into Ivy League schools. The educators run the local schools with this in view because if they didn't, the parents would fire them. And the parents are then run by the educators to conform with the pattern of demand. Very large numbers of the kids live accordingly. This has all sorts of implications, including the fact that they don't have much leisure time. These are very busy kids from the time they enter school."

Kahn went on to describe other teen-age cultural subgroups:

• *The hoodlums,* young people who manage to break out of the rat-race pattern to develop their own version of hoodlumism. They call one another "hoods" and are recognized as such by other youngsters. Their delinquencies could be regarded as moderate, but they do their best to call attention to themselves as troublemakers.

• *The "peace corps,"* which overlaps considerably with the rat-race pack and only slightly with the hoodlums. These are youngsters involved in such movements as civil rights protests or demonstrations for a variety of causes.

• *The "Barbie and Ken" imitators,* so named for the popular dolls. This probably is the largest group and overlaps the rat-racers to some extent. These youngsters "eventually model themselves on the 'in' families. They become miniature versions of what their parents are. . . . These are the kids who buy a value system which says that what you can get away with is more important than what is right. This is part of the business ethic that they also inherit from the adult community and which is reinforced in various ways by school systems."

• *The "cool and dull" kids,* who play it safe to the extreme. Being unable to make the rat race, they withdraw. They do not have what it takes to become Ken or Barbie, and they are afraid to be hoodlums. So they follow the path of moderation, becoming social and intellectual underachievers.

The experts brought together by the Children's Bureau tended to accept the fact that the greatest majority of our adolescents are just average kids who go through school without attracting much attention and then emerge into the world to live out their lives without making a ripple in the water.

Some concern was expressed lest these members of the cool and dull generation never learn their own identities or find out "who, if anyone, wants *me?*" But more concern was voiced for the large numbers of young people who become so disappointed and frustrated that they seek the kind of outlet afforded on the Florida beaches every spring or at hippie hangouts.

The Easter weekend frolics every year provide a brief outlet for the young people who want to let off steam, and while they are an annoyance to many adults, they certainly should not be cause for alarm. However, the hippies and runaways give us all something to worry about. In 1966, more than 90,000 juvenile runaways were picked up by the police, and almost half of them were girls. The New York City police alone received about 9,000 calls from parents in the metropolitan area asking for help in finding runaway teen-agers. About twice that many inquiries were made from out of town and out of state.

"Statistics are hard to come by, but there is reason to believe that as many as half a million kids left home last year [1966]," it was estimated by Rabbi Samuel Schrage, assistant executive director of the New York City Youth Board. "And there are thousands of parents all over the country who haven't heard from their kids for months. This creates terrific problems."

There always have been many runaways from homes in impoverished slums and ghettos, Schrage pointed out, but the youngsters leaving home today come increasingly from middle-class families. "Too many middle-class parents are too cock-sure of themselves," he explained. "They say 'It can't happen to me,' but it does. And once gone, it's easier to find a pedigreed dog in this country than a runaway kid."

Another social worker with many years of experience with youngsters, Chessor Bowles, retired head counselor at William Sloane House, a residence hotel operated in New York by the YMCA, has observed that "some of these kids are running for their lives. I've talked to all kinds, including plenty from Ivy League colleges and the Social Register. Their problems are different from the rest. Some of them are being slowly smothered to death. They're trying to cut the apron strings, to accomplish something, anything on their own. It's hard [for parents] to understand because frequently they don't understand it themselves and express their anger and despair in very subtle ways."

In San Francisco, whose Haight-Ashbury district is the capital of Hippieland, Jim Fouratt, a twenty-three-year-old hippie leader and dropout from Harvard University, told an interviewer that his fellow hippies were "very strung-out kids with individual hang-ups."

Those runaways who will talk about their problems give a variety of reasons why they left home. "My mother kept bugging me about school and staying out late," said sixteen-year-old Martie. After a year of living in Greenwich Village with her boyfriend, she sees no point in returning to school "until there's something I really need to learn."

When Norman was seventeen he dropped out of an Ivy League college and went to New York to try to "make it on my own." "My father pulled every string he could, argued with me, threatened me, but I stayed, I had to stay." After a year in the city, he decided to return to school, on his own terms. "I'm going back now because *I* want to, not to please my father. I had to find out first if I could make it on my own."

Teen-agers interviewed about their running away seemed to feel that their parents were domineering, lacking in understanding, and overly intent on having their own way. On the other hand, some parents regarded their teen-agers as thoughtless, self-centered, and immature—a threat to their own control of a situation.

Tragic situations can and do develop in Hippieland, the most sensational of which was the 1967 murder of Linda Fitzpatrick, the eighteen-year-old daughter of a wealthy spice importer she left an exclusive girls' school and ran away from her family's thirty-room, $155,000 Connecticut mansion to live a sordid, hand-to-mouth existence in Greenwich Village. Linda, described by her friends as a girl who "had everything," and her hippie boyfriend were murdered in a filthy tenement basement.

"She seemed perfectly normal," a Connecticut friend said. "But how do you know unless you know someone well? We all grow up together here in Greenwich, but when we go to boarding school, we come back and we're probably different. It's very easy to put up a front back here and cover the bumps. I'm not saying Linda had the bumps, but she may have had and no one would really have known."

The authorities and psychiatrists agree that many of the young people who smother their own identities by living in squalor and donning the uniform of the hippie and who preach love while really hating what they are doing are in need of psychiatric help. One of these was Pamela Rae Koeppel, a fourteen-year-old schoolgirl who ran away from her Long Island home and was found in a Greenwich Village hotel after her distraught father had walked the streets searching for her. Adolph Koeppel, a prosperous lawyer, told policemen that she had been a "disturbed child" and had been seeing a psychiatrist. He and his wife thought her problems were under control, and so apparently did her psychiatrist, and she was given a summer off from therapy. But when fall came, Pamela lost interest in school and began seeing her psychiatrist again. At the same time, the girl became interested in the hippies and the flower children. She started wearing "hippie" beads and painted a blue flower on her cheek. And then she ran away.

The runaways and the hippies are one result of the monumental pressures on youngsters. When they cannot stand any more, some of them leave, and their bewildered parents wonder why. In addition to making impossible demands, parents in many cases do not know how to allow and encourage their youngsters to accept responsibility. They do not seem to know how to *give* responsibility to youth. At some point, parents have to bring themselves to be able to determine what kinds of tasks they are willing to entrust to young people. They need to ask themselves what kinds of decisions they are willing to have teen-agers make. How much are they going to allow them to say about shaping their own lives and the institutions that serve them? Are they going to give them a choice to *be* themselves?

This brings us back to the parents of the young suicide, the boy who killed himself because he could not stand to be a failure in his parents' eyes. His were among the countless overaspiring parents who are becoming stumbling blocks to the growth of their children. This sort of parent, acting out of the best and most sincere of motives, wants his children to rise above his own station in life; he wants them to have more and better education, which often means going to a "good" school. Actually, it means to them excelling in everything, regardless of whether "everything" is what the children want to do—or are able to do.

Youngsters already confronted with unprecedented competition with their peers at school are prodded and pushed by parents competing with one another to rear children who are the most popular, most talented, brightest, etc., etc., etc. If a youngster does not measure up, he is branded an underachiever by his overaspiring parents, who place unnecessary, unrealistic, and sometimes unbearable burdens on him by being unable to accept him for what he *is*. It is important for a parent to try to remember that what *he* wants his child to do is worthless unless it is within the realm of the child's abilities and interests. One feels justified in asking: What makes a parent think he has any grounds for expecting his children to be more than he is?

It should not be necessary to have to point out that not every youngster belongs in college—and that includes those who win admittance. As one who has been on the board of a small college, I have seen at first hand what excessive pressure can do. One consequence is the high dropout rate and another is the imposition of shortsighted educational standards on our society.

Although not typical, one wrongly aspiring mother comes to mind in this connection. She was a devoutly religious woman who wanted more than anything else in the world for her son to enter the priesthood. Contrary to his wishes, he complied, entered a seminary at a young age, and eventually was ordained. After he had served the church steadfastly for many years, his mother died. Only then did he begin to realize how lonely he was, how unhappy he had become with his vocation, and how much he yearned for the companionship of a family. While he was able to understand why he felt as he did, he was helpless to do anything about it except to drown his disappointments in alcohol. Not even the memory of his mother could sustain him, and in time he became a hopeless drunkard, unable to fulfill his priestly functions. Eventually he was sent to a mental hospital and there he remains.

In cases such as this—as well as in less extreme instances—the motivations of the parents and their attitudes toward their own lives become vital to the children. In a sense the need for achievement and competition in our culture sabotages creativity and spontaneity. The American dream is to make more money each year and buy a bigger car with part of the proceeds. By and large, our school system is geared to this, thus limiting and in some cases destroying the spirit of creativity of the classroom.

Tom's story is a good example of how children can become the victims of their parents' striving wishes—i.e., demands. From the age of ten, he was fascinated with automobiles—far more so than the average boy. At fourteen he was mechanically skilled enough to dismantle and reassemble an automobile engine. He decided he wanted to be an auto mechanic and would train for that after he finished high school.

Needless to say, that was not what his parents, particularly his mother, had in mind. As residents of a well-to-do community, she and her husband keenly felt the social competition with their neighbors. The mother, a graduate of one of the more prestigious women's colleges, was deeply engrossed in the theater and the arts. She was counting on Tom to attend college and seek a profession in writing, law, or medicine. Certainly, the idea of his becoming "just an auto mechanic" had not occurred to her.

Tom's interest in cars and engines pleased her at first; she felt it demonstrated that he had manual dexterity and imagination, and it gave her something to brag about to her friends. When he started talking about wanting to be an auto mechanic, she laughed it off as a "phase" he was passing through. As for Tom's father, he was away on business or on the golf course much of the time and did not get involved in the details of his son's life beyond inquiring about his grades, how he was "making out" with the girls, and whether he had won a basketball letter yet.

Then one day Tom's mother awakened to the realization that the boy meant what he said about his plans for the future, and she went to work with a vengeance to try to coerce him into becoming what *she* thought he ought to be. First came a common form of parental bribery. She offered him a new car or a summer tour of Europe if he would promise to go to college. Tom mistakenly interpreted these as proposals he was free to accept or reject; he thought he really had a choice. So, because tinkering with old jalopies was more appealing to him than driving a new car or visiting European art galleries, he politely refused his mother's offer without realizing its purpose.

That made her increasingly anxious. Because her own conception of herself was based on her competition with her neighbors, she felt increasingly that her son *had* to "succeed," which meant his following the academic trail that many of his classmates were being shepherded—or dragged—along by their parents, *and* his doing what was meaningful to *her*.

Thus began a two-year war of attrition. "Do you want to be a failure?" his mother would ask in tones ranging from whines to accusations and rage. "A boy with your background must make something of himself." "How can you do this to me?" "Why can't you be like other boys?" "Do you want your father and me to be the disgrace of the neighborhood?"

On and on it went. At first Tom ignored the pressures and tears, but eventually the matter began to prey on his mind; his mother had succeeded in brainwashing him. He wanted to say "No," but he found that he could not. He became angry, but could find no way to express his feeling. Every time he started to say something, he was overcome by guilt. He became depressed. Later he told me how he used to say to himself, "Why can't she understand how I feel?" Gradually he went into a decline, slipping to a point where he actually came to regard his own ambitions as wrong and condemned himself for them. He was convinced he was no good. He stopped working on cars, stayed away from his friends, kept to himself, and did nothing but mope.

By the time Tom's teachers were able to persuade his mother that he needed professional help and he had paid his first visit to me, the boy seemed to be interested in nothing. It did not take long for me to realize that underneath his mask was a seething mass of anger and frustration. I found it necessary to see his mother, too, as often as I saw him, for she had to be convinced that her son was a person, not an extension of herself, and that she was passing on to him her own frustrations and insecurities. In fact, she was making him bear the full brunt of her own inadequacies.

The situation has a Biblical analogy in the admonition of St. Paul in one of his epistles that different people have different abilities. All have a contribution to make and all are deserving of respect regardless of where their attributes lie. Tom's mother had not been able to see this, but gradually, over a period of many months, she came to realize her mistakes and feel guilty enough about them to repair at least some of the damage. At the same time, Tom matured in counseling to a point where he decided he would go to college to study automotive engineering, a solution so obvious I still wonder why his parents had not suggested it themselves in the first place. Tom said he would give college a "try." His mother agreed that if after a year he did not want to finish she would accept his decision to become an auto mechanic, if that was what he really wanted to do. They were communicating at last!

There is no reason to question the intentions of the parents of the Toms of the world. While they may give in to the pressures of society, they are trying at the same time to make an honest effort to do what is best for their children. However, largely out of their desire to be good parents they frequently become too rigid, losing both their sense of humor and their sense of proportion. While parents certainly have a right, and even a responsibility, to demand that teen-agers conform, at least to a degree, they must also give them enough freedom to experience many things for themselves and must refrain from treating them as pieces of personal property. The teen-ager is, after all, only trying to assert himself, whether by refusing to take a bath, by performing ridiculous dances, or even by deciding to become a mechanic. While the latter choice is perhaps of more consequence in the long run, all are efforts at self-expression. Youngsters are members of a subculture in which they are trying to say, "We no longer belong to the world of the child and yet we are not ready for the adult world, so we must have a society of our own." To interfere with this is to stunt a child in an important period of growth.

The stories of two men and their shaggy-haired sons illustrate this. One, a crew-cut type, nagged his son to have his hair cropped short, too, even though it no longer was the style in teen-age circles. The boy rebelled. He wanted his hair even longer; it was the thing to do. Actually he had not been wearing his hair very long, but it was not so short as his father's. His father was so concerned lest his son let his hair grow as long as some other boys were wearing theirs that he continued to demand that the boy conform to his own tonsorial concept. Consequently the son let his hair grow even longer. Had his father allowed him freedom within limits, this probably would not have happened.

The second father dealt with a similar situation in a different—and more effective—fashion without saying a word. His boy let his hair grow to his shoulders at a time when this was the height of teen-age masculine style. Neither parent said a word, difficult as it was to sit across the dinner table from him every night, silently wishing he would at least comb or wash the unmanageable snarls once in a while. Finally the father decided he had had enough. He went to a store, bought a frilly dress, and hung it in his son's closet. Nothing was said, but the next day the boy visited a barber. The dress disappeared. As far as I know, to this day the matter has never been discussed. I will wager that someday the father and son will have a good laugh over the incident.

The style adopted by many boys who let their hair grow in the late 1960's may have been related to sexual confusion as well as rebellion. But there also is an element of conformity in such fads. The self-styled rebels actually conform in a sense by following the dictates of their subculture rather than by becoming the individuals they think they are. All beatniks, for example, look pretty much alike; they identify with one another. So it is with the hippies, too. They are different from most of the rest of society, but within their subculture they are in uniform while engaged in a mass protest against the conformity of their elders.

Sometimes we adults forget that adolescents have certain rights to exist as individual personalities. This does not mean that there are no limits to the bounds of the freedom to which they are entitled, of course. But if they feel they are being "different" in conforming to some of the practices of their sub-culture, they have a right to this difference—within reason. Youngsters also crave the right of privacy, the right to find refuge in their own room or work area without being interrupted or criticized. They should have the right of decision, up to a point and within the general family rules laid down for them. They have a right to choose many aspects of their own clothing, their own friends, their own intellectual pursuits, all of these choices, of course, being within the framework of certain standards; but these standards depend entirely on the parents. If the guidelines are there, they will often be followed.

Yes, our youngsters need and deserve a Bill of Rights of their own. Along with it I would suggest several guidelines for coping with the problems of teen-agers and for making life with them and for them more bearable. Here are a few ideas:

• There are times when it is necessary to show your adolescent child that you trust him, even when you may deem his judgments faulty. This does not mean that the foolish decisions he makes should be overlooked, but since the youngster is developing and learning and since he is unsure of his position, he needs to know that his parents have enough faith in him to let him make—and learn from—his own mistakes.

He also would like to feel that his parents are aware of his point of view and his position, and it should be obvious that he needs consistency from his elders. When a child does something calling for punishment, he generally knows it. Therefore he becomes confused if his father, for example, is ambivalent about punishment or does not apply it directly.

I am reminded of John. He entered therapy when he was

thirty-two years old. In the course of developing his psychological history, I noted an incident in his early adolescence
that kept coming to his mind. It seems that he and several
other youngsters had stolen a small item from a five-and-ten-
cent store. When his father learned about it, he did not provide a firm, just, and realistic form of punishment, but said
something to the effect that "I know you realize you have
made a mistake that has hurt *me* and I know you won't do it
again."

In manhood, John still was disturbed by this incident because he now realized his father had not reacted appropriately.
"Why didn't my father punish me in some way that made
sense?" John wondered. What he was really asking was: "Why
didn't my father love me enough to teach me the right way?"
or "Why was he so caught up in his own identity problem
that he was unable to deal with the reality of the situation?"

• A little praise of adolescents once in a while goes a long
way toward building their inner strengths. It is important for
parents to try to look at the positive side of things and give
their children the support and confidence they need by com-
plimenting their strong points as well as criticizing their weak
ones.

Instead of saying, "You made only one A on your report
card. Why couldn't you do better?" a positive approach might
be, "Why, you received an A in history! That's wonderful!
Maybe you have special talents in that subject and should develop them." It might spark a youngster to do better in other
subjects if he is praised for showing excellence in one.

• A child needs encouragement to develop his own value
system, using yours as a guide rather than a blueprint. While

your value system may be acceptable to you, your child is another person, and if he is forced to adhere to yours, he may go through life as though wearing an ill-fitting suit; moreover, he may find himself unable to make decisions for himself. In developing a value system, a person must learn to assume responsibility for his own thoughts, deeds, and decisions. This is an area in which many parents fall short, partly because of their failures to develop well-defined systems of values of their own and to assume responsibility for their own actions at home, in society, or at the office. For instance, a child is caught cheating in a school examination. He cannot understand why he is punished. In discussing it with his counselor, he says, "My daddy brags about cheating on his income tax return and isn't punished. Why should I have to pay for *this?*"

• When a child becomes an adolescent, his parents should be able to accept the fact that the time is coming when they will have to let him go—or, rather, let go of him. This is the time for them to encourage him to begin working out his problems of separation from them with the knowledge that eventually he will become independent. However, it is possible to impose too much responsibility on children at too early an age; it is just as bad to cut a child off when he still needs emotional support as it is to make him overly dependent. Premature separation may produce an excessive sense of responsibility that can plague a person throughout his life. It may even cause him to try to take on responsibilities he can never fulfill and thus live in a constant state of frustration in which he so consistently falls short of his self-demands that he can never accept his own limitations.

If I were to sum up the problems of adolescents in one sentence, I would say that it is the tension between the struggle for independence and an inclination to remain dependent. This has always been a human problem. What it boils down to is one question: Are we willing and able to grow up?

This was the paramount question in the student demonstrations on college campuses in recent years, most notably at Columbia University, where student demonstrators provided a dramatic and discouraging example of the degree to which a teen-ager can be both child and adult. The demonstrations also showed what can happen when young people lose self-control in exercising self-expression.

The most wanton and destructive of all the student protests thus far in our country occurred in a senseless outburst at Columbia in May of 1968, when students acted without concern for persons or property and without respect for democratic processes. Theirs was, in fact, a revolution rather than a protest, with some of the leaders acknowledging that their goal was much more than reform.

Marshall McLuhan, the professor with controversial views on the use of the communications media, applied his theories to the problem of violence in an interview after the Columbia rioting. He came to the conclusion that violence is an involuntary quest for identity. "Violence," he said, "is directed toward image-making, not goals. The Columbia students have no goals, neither do the Negroes. As long as we provide them with new technology, they must struggle for a new image. . . . The discrepancy between the riches of the TV feast and the poverty of the school experience is creating great ferment, friction and psychic violence."

The identity crisis posed at Columbia—and at other schools

as well—has been compounded by an outdated, inflexible academic system, by the Vietnam war, by the knowledge explosion, by the pressures of affluence, and by inconsistent parental values. In this sort of situation an adolescent is likely to accept the leadership of anyone who offers him an outlet for his confusion, frustration, and anger. At Columbia, those in the clutches of such confusion followed the leadership of a small group of students who took matters into their own hands.

Two special qualities stand out in the student sheep who followed the riot leaders. One was their disregard for the property or the rights of others. They behaved as a small child does during the period in his life when he feels he is the only person in the world whose wishes, desires, and needs are to be considered.

The second quality that stood out among the rioting students was their unwillingness to accept responsibility for their acts. After they had wrecked laboratories, destroyed years of valuable research papers, and desecrated offices and classrooms, their cries for clemency became a denial of their ability to face the consequences of what they had done.

It is interesting to note also that the student demonstrations on many campuses have been intensified by the ambivalence of the institutions in dealing with them effectively. Institutions that have taken quick, decisive positions have suffered the least from student upheavals; those that have been slow to move or were ambivalent once they took action have faced recurrent student unrest.

Young people—and many adults, too—need a strong and definitive father figure, even though it may be one with which they strongly disagree. Praise and punishment, properly and wisely administered, are important; there is something reassuring and comforting in knowing "where Daddy stands" and that he means what he says.

All of us know adults who in reality are still children, just as we know teen-agers who are old far beyond their years. Some of those who are unable to assume the realistic responsibilities of the adult world have been the victims of parents who could not distinguish between themselves and their children, and thus regarded their children as extensions of themselves. Such a mistake is made in the guise of love, in whose name we often commit crimes against our children that can hamper their efforts to achieve their own sense of identity.

Yet we should never underrate the value of *caring* in child-rearing. This was dramatized in studies made by the psychologist Renée Spitz in orphanages in Chile, where children who received the basic needs of life—food, clothing, and a place to sleep—died or became retarded because adequate individual care was not possible. At the other extreme, we are faced in our country with a situation in which the importance of a child in the home tends to be overvalued; everything is focused on him, with parents regarding any criticism or disciplinary action—taken by someone else—to be an attack on themselves. Although many teachers discipline children in a poor way—largely because of their own problems—we also know that in many instances a student deserves the scolding or punishment meted out in class.

We often see parents of a child who has been disciplined become irate because the teacher has "questioned the actions of *my* little boy." When this happens the child may grow up with the notion that he will always be protected. When he goes into the world, he finds that is not the case, and he is faced with a whole new—and unnecessary—set of problems. He is now plunged into a technological culture in which he becomes a number, often depersonalized in his work, with few tools for developing a sense of identity. He is a living, breathing, walking, talking IBM punchcard, his days of teenage self-expression only a memory unless he has in his own way naturally established his sense of identity so that he may be able to keep his balance in the impersonal business world. How a youngster gets through the struggle for his own independence and identity—and in the long run, survival—depends on how secure he feels, how much support he receives from his parents, and, of course, his own make-up.

Even a child who is relatively secure is at times rebellious. It is always amazing to observe the anxieties of insecure parents who feel that even the most innocent forms of rebellion are directed against them as persons. A child who never rebels is not likely to be able to break away from his parents sufficiently to establish his own identity.

It seems absurd for parents to go on demanding that their children should love them just because they are *their* children. The Biblical injunction "Honor thy father and thy mother" is misinterpreted by many. "To honor" is quite different from "to love," but we find parents feeling *they* must love their children because they *are* theirs, and children feeling *they* must love their parents simply because they *are* their parents. Well, it just does not work that way—necessarily. Perhaps all of us would have fewer problems if we used the words "honor," "respect," and "care," and let love enter as a natural by-product. Love is a marvelous force, the most constructive force in the world. But to be effective, love must come naturally and spontaneously, not because there is a rule that says you "must" or "should" love. Out of honor and respect, love may come, but they are not synonymous. When parents and children really love one another, it is wonderful to behold, but when the idea of "love" springs from coercion and a desire for control, it can be destructive.

5

Some People Never
Do Grow Up

Immaturity is by no means limited to teen-agers. Our emotionally "retarded" adult population is responsible for the highest divorce rate in history. Divorce is an admission of failure; but it is something more, too. Almost invariably the failure that leads to divorce is a result of immaturity, a poor sense of self-worth.

Divorce can be a failure of two people to develop the ability to *give* rather than merely to take. This is a kind of immaturity.

It can be a failure to realize that everyone does not see the world in the same way, particularly in the way *you* see it—another sign of immaturity.

It can also be a failure of two people to communicate to each other what their real feelings and needs are. Problems often result. Immaturity enters here, too.

There are many kinds of failure expressed in the one out of every four marriages that ends in divorce. Added to these are the near failures, the one or two out of every four marriages that teeter on the brink of divorce. The causes of these failures are many.

One human failure that wrecks or threatens marriages is the inability of a husband and wife to respect each other's right to privacy, which is necessary even in the most intimate relationship. Another is the failure resulting from being unable to recognize or accept the fact that people remain basically pretty much the same after marriage as they were before. You are wasting your breath if you say, "I'm going to change Harry after we are married," or "She won't get away with *that* after she becomes my wife." Many a husband and wife have come to me complaining about traits of their spouses. When I ask if this trait existed before marriage, the answer almost invariably is, "Yes, but I thought I could change him (her)." I have to tell them that while a man or woman can change in the course of marriage, it is a mistake to think that one can enter a marriage with the idea that he can change his partner.

One of the most serious marital problems encountered in counseling is the inability to see the world from another person's point of view. Some people cling to the notion that *everything* is just the way they see it, that no one else feels or sees things differently. Ed and Jane B. are a good example of this attitude. They came to me for marriage counseling because, even though they had been divorced for five years, they found that they were unable to stay away from each other. They still shared a bank account and met regularly, and they thought a reconciliation seemed possible.

Jane, an attractive professional woman in her forties, came to see me first. She told me that Ed, a skilled technician, came from a culturally deprived background, while she was a college graduate, and as a result he had always felt inadequate. "He wants to be constantly on the move," she said. "He changes jobs and we have moved to different parts of the country. I would prefer to stay put, but he gets moody when he isn't moving about." There were other complaints. She felt he constantly belittled her; they argued over money; he ignored her friends; she had to prepare all his meals for him and wash the dishes even though she worked; he lied to her and would not discuss his problems with her, and he was too close to his parents.

That was quite an indictment. It made me wonder why in the world she and Ed were even thinking about a reconciliation. But I kept listening to her and eventually it all came out. At the root of her complaints was her still-smoldering resentment over an affair her husband had been involved in ten years before she had even met him. Although the romance was over long before Ed came into her life, she still resented it because she could not help but feel that somehow she had never measured up to the other girl in his estimation. As is often the case, the problems Jane presented were not the real difficulties that had caused the marriage to founder.

With my encouragement, Jane persuaded Ed to come to see me, too, and we had a number of marriage counseling sessions. From the outset they were unable to discuss their differences candidly with each other because each had a set opinion about the world and would not budge. To the final hour of counseling, each insisted "It has to be *my* way." Ed wanted to be accepted as he was, to be treated as a man, to be loved, to take his place in the marriage, and to be respected and supported in his part of an effort to share and to work together. Jane steadfastly—perhaps even stubbornly—stuck to her refusal to accompany him again if he should be transferred or moved to take another new job. She said she could not accept him if she found out that he had had an affair with another woman since their divorce, and she still was bothered by what she considered to be his untruthfulness.

In short, both refused to move from their respective sides of the marital iron curtain. It became obvious that there could be no reconciliation without conciliation; the basic problem was not so much that the marriage could not be repaired as that they were unable to part emotionally even though they were legally divorced.

Added to this was their inability to communicate in a meaningful way. They thought that because they used the same words or because each knew his own meaning, the other also knew what was intended, while in actuality they had completely different outlooks and emotional reactions.

Unfortunately, Ed never really accepted the idea of marriage counseling; he came only because he felt he had to. Jane finally decided not to see him or talk to him on the telephone for several weeks, a strategy that served only to make him resentful. He interpreted her silence as collusion between Jane and me, and he accused me of being on her "side." Further marriage counseling became impossible, and the couple remained apart, with nothing resolved, still suffering from their immaturity.

Harriet and Wilbur V. also had their problems. Their marriage had been damaged by Wilbur's affair with an extremely aggressive woman who was determined to marry him. Wilbur was an outwardly easygoing man who showed the world a facade of forthrightness and an apparently logical approach to life. On the surface he was a nice, attractive person, the kind much sought-after for social engagements. But beneath his gregarious exterior, Wilbur seethed with anxieties, and, unconsciously at least, he defended himself against them by trying to be extremely logical and reasonable.

His wife, on the other hand, dealt with her emotions by being a super-*feeling* woman, reacting to everything on an emotional level, laughing or crying too much, too loud, and too often. If something did not suit Harriet's purposes, she wept and wailed, while Wilbur conducted himself as though he was a district attorney gathering all the facts in "the case."

Harriet was basically passive behind her mask of histrionics, and both she and Wilbur had a tremendous need to please each other. The moment a point of discord arose, however, one of them would take it personally, begin to feel defensive, and then proceed to try to prove he or she was right. So, when he started playing district attorney with his logic, and she emoted, true communication stopped, although torrents of words poured forth. It became so important for both of them to be right that they simply could no longer communicate.

This kind of breakdown is a symptom of deeper problems. Here we have two people who remained so self-centered that they could not communicate with each other—a form of immaturity. Naturally no one has the right to demand that his mate be "mature" before marriage. As a matter of fact, if that were a prerequisite almost no marriages would take place! Nor would it make sense for one to insist that both be on the same level of emotional development. However, the ability of two people to *hear* one another and to accept their mutual rights to their own personalities goes a long way toward setting the stage for a successful marriage.

The very word "marriage" implies the sharing of the experiences of life. It means that in taking the marriage vow, the partners are stating a willingness to be concerned about each other's needs and wants. Simply stated, a person has to be able to give as well as to take in order to contribute to a successful marriage.

Delayed adolescence, or at least a continuance of it, can persist through the adult years, making a true marriage difficult, perhaps impossible. This immaturity is manifested in many ways, principally in sexual problems, financial problems, and in-law problems.

What is meant by maturity? One of its important facets is the ability to be able to give as well as to take, to step outside oneself and accept other ways of seeing the world, to be flexible enough to accept change. Only a foolish husband or wife thinks the emotional range of the relationship that existed when the "I do's" were exchanged is bound to continue forever. We are told that the honeymoon is over after a period of time—the first, second, or third year, perhaps. Some say the seventh year is the "most difficult," some the tenth, and so on. What are they saying? That there comes a time when a couple become aware that their relationship is not the same as it was when they were married. The "difficult year" can be one of trial because it is then that you either make your adjustments or flirt with failure. To what do you adjust? If you are so rigid that you think this is the last adjustment you will have to make, you are likely to encounter another "difficult year," and another, and perhaps many more.

Speaking generally, the successful marriage is one in which a husband and wife are able to adjust to the idea that their relationship is constantly developing and changing, and, it is to be hoped, growing. Rather than thinking it will be "this way" forever and ever, they accept an evolution in their relationship as inevitable, particularly with the bearing of children, getting a new job, making more money, moving to a new home, and so on. Those who are able to adjust to the fact that the only permanent thing in life is change are bound to stand a better chance of success in marriage.

Sex is a natural component of the marriage failure that is expressed in divorce. Immaturity often is at the root of sexual problems. We live in an era of considerable sexual freedom and open discussions of sex, which is good in many ways. People are much franker about sex in marriage than they used to be, but despite what we say and know, many—if not most—of us have been reared in a puritanical tradition, at least in respect to sex, and often we find ourselves in conflict between what we want to do and the way we were taught.

Oddly enough, talk about sex is being accompanied by an apparent effort to desexualize sex. This has become obvious in some of the highly publicized activities that ostensibly flaunt freedom of sexual expression. While some of these have contributed greatly to creating an open and often adult perspective on sex, some also have removed part of the sexuality from sex, so that it frequently becomes a sort of spectator sport. An attitude of look, but don't touch, or don't take it seriously is often the result. This juvenile approach to sex has as its ultimate purpose the encouragement of fantasy about sex, with the fantasy threatening to become more important than actual sex. This desexualization of sex adds a new dimension to the identity crisis.

In marriage, sexual maladjustment often becomes a problem, or at least the problem that is taken to a counselor. This was *the* difficulty as far as Mrs. A. P. was concerned when she came to me for help. She was overly jealous and convinced that her husband was not only being unfaithful but also taunting her emotionally by making her feel inadequate. Their marriage was on the verge of breaking up as a result. An attractive, thirty-one-year-old woman, Mrs. A. P. was pregnant when she married, and she and her husband had only the one child, although originally they had hoped for more. She had come from a large family in which she was the last of six children, two boys and four girls. The children were expected to perform household chores as soon as they were old enough, and she felt as though she had been working all her life. Her childhood seemed to have been lacking in companionship and understanding, from siblings or parents. She felt that she had received no direction, although as the youngest child she was "bossed" constantly. Her ego development seemed poor as a result. She was one of those who asked, in a sense, "Who am I, really?"

What exactly is the ego and why does it get us involved in so many of our psychological difficulties? The ego is the part of our personality that gives us the ability and strength to integrate many of our feelings. It helps us to recognize and stand aside from our fantasies and from the feelings projected on us by others. And it also helps us to come to terms with the baser aspects of our own personalities, in other words enabling us to "live with ourselves."

When I say that Mrs. A. P. appeared to have a poor ego development, I mean that although she was intelligent and outwardly pleasant, she was obviously immature in her inability to interpret her own feelings and those projected by her husband without suffering from a constant dread of being abandoned, which was the one thing she both feared and yet almost wanted. Mrs. A. P. still suffered from strong feelings of remorse about having been pregnant before marriage. Although she tried to discuss sex in sophisticated terms, it was obvious that her background and training had been somewhat strict and that there was a conflict between what she thought she should feel and what she actually felt about sex. She seemed to realize that her ego limits were weak, and this awareness in itself gave her enough strength to seek help.

Unfortunately her husband, despite his apparent strengths, also was passive, expecting her to take the initiative in their everyday activities, thus sparing him from as many responsibilities as possible. His was a classic kind of passivity, which can best be described as an inability to initiate action in his own behalf, so that he went through life as a kind of hitchhiker, always getting a free ride and letting someone else do the steering. This is another way of saying that such a passive person wants to be taken care of long after he should be and to far too great a degree.

Because Mr. and Mrs. A. P. had inner problems of their own that needed solving before they could try to mend their marriage, I suggested that she enter into individual therapy. When she insisted on concentrating on the marriage, I confronted her with her own ambivalence about wanting to be taken care of and playing a little girl role while at the same time making an effort to be a wife and mother; she cried out both for the setting of limits and the right to do what she pleased *when* she pleased. Specifically, she wanted the right to continue to indulge herself in temper tantrums even though she knew she was too old for such childish behavior. It became apparent that she hoped I would help her set appropriate limits for the expression of her infantile rage, but at the same time she fought against accepting any limits.

Mrs. A. P. worked hard at trying to sort out and solve her problems. Eventually she began to understand some of the childhood feelings that still plagued her. She realized how much she resented the strict demands made on her as a small child and the necessity of having had to share parental love with her brothers and sisters. More important, she began to understand that regardless of how angry she became, she could never turn back the clock so that her parents could right the wrongs—real and imagined—she recalled from her childhood. She began to see that she would win respect only if she respected herself, and as she began to develop a better concept of her own worth her husband's immaturity became less of a threat to her. Her improved feelings about herself—her strengthened ego—enabled Mrs. A. P. to remain married and her situation at home was greatly improved.

Sex had been the first thing she had discussed with me, but this was not really the problem. While the first words spoken to a marriage counselor often are "My wife (husband) does not understand me," sex often is the problem given as the reason for seeking counseling, as was the case with Mrs. A. P. Generally so-called sexual incompatibility is a symptom of something else, something much deeper within either or both parties, as we have seen. Complaints involving sex may include disagreement on frequency of intercourse, inability to react sexually the way a spouse thinks one should, a desire by one for sexual behavior that is repugnant to the other, and extramarital relationships.

It would be naive and even ludicrous to gainsay that sex is a very important part of marriage, although there have been some apparently successful unions where there was little or no sexual activity. While it is very important, sex by itself does not necessarily "make" a marriage. Shared interests, aims, and goals and mutual respect also are vital ingredients.

Infrequency of sexual relations was the "presenting problem" when Mr. and Mrs. B. sought counseling as a last resort when their fifteen-year childless marriage was breaking up. He had left home to live with another woman but was constantly faced with ambivalent feelings; he did not know what he really wanted or who he really was. In counseling it developed that he occasionally was impotent and his wife sometimes bordered on frigidity.

Four months after we had been meeting once a week, I asked Mrs. B. what she thought she had done to influence her husband to seek affection from another woman. To my surprise, she replied: "I'm sure I was partly to blame." At first she was unable to pinpoint any particular attitude or action that might have sent her husband to another woman's bed, but as she talked it became apparent that she saw herself in constant competition with Mr. B. She had to "beat him to the punch" in retaliation for what she regarded as his constant criticism of her.

Mr. B., on the other hand, had sold himself "a bill of goods," convincing himself that he was a democratic "ruler" of his marriage. He vacillated between telling her what to do and kidding himself into thinking that he was allowing her to make up her own mind. Yet, it was difficult for him to take responsibility for his actions. He was immature.

The couple apparently spent a great deal of time discussing their problems when they were alone. One day they came in with a list of grievances they had compiled and discussed, which indicated they were sincere in trying to reach a reconciliation. But here again there was a contest, a constant game one had to win and the other lose. She was annoyed because he was always late; he retorted that she took too long to prepare meals, get dressed to go out, etc. They finally came to recognize their behavior as an expression of resistance to being with each other. She saw him as a perfectionist who expected everything to be done in a certain prescribed way, and she "got even" by being unresponsive sexually; in fact, sex became a chore for her. This in turn became a threat to him, to his security and his very manhood. When she was willing to engage in intercourse, he retaliated with impotence, and their dilemma eventually became so great that in order to reassure himself of his manhood he found another woman.

Often we are inclined as outsiders to sympathize entirely with the woman whose husband is philandering without considering the possibility that he may have been driven to this course, as Mr. B. was, by circumstances not entirely of his making. It probably is safe to say that the instances of adultery that are entirely the fault of one marriage partner are extremely rare, if, indeed, there are any at all.

There were some other facets of Mr. and Mrs. B.'s troubles that might contribute to further understanding of shaky marriages. Eventually it became possible for them to learn to compromise on matters ranging from where to have dinner to when to have sexual relations. They discussed at length such questions as: How do you arrive at a decision for action when no compromise is possible? How do you arrive at compromise when one *is* possible? How can you compromise without losing your self-respect?

There also was the matter of his learning to say "Yes" or "No" and meaning it. In the past he had acted the way some parents do with small children, telling her she absolutely could not spend $150 for a cat and then taking her to a pet shop to buy one. He became convinced that there were times he had to say "No" and mean it and also that he would have to learn to explain his refusal in kind terms.

This couple really worked hard at trying to mend their marriage. Eventually each entered individual counseling when it became clear to them that their difficulties were largely within themselves, not the marriage. This actually is a kind of marriage counseling, for if people can benefit as individuals, the marriage also may be helped. If the partners in marriage learn to know themselves better they will also come to understand the marriage.

However, most people seeking marriage counseling usually have already decided on divorce and look for help only as a last resort. Under the divorce law enacted in New York in

1967, all divorcing couples are required to go through a course of counseling. This has created an entirely new dimension of counseling, because many who become involved in it have no wish to repair the marriage but rather are merely complying with the law in order to get a divorce. Their relationships have deteriorated to the point where they simply cannot tolerate one another, and counseling is pointless.

Counseling *can* and does save some marriages, particularly if couples seek help early. After the divorce or separation papers are filed it is usually a little late, however. In any case, there is no disgrace in having marriage problems and in seeking a third party who will listen objectively.

There is no rule, nor should there be, that marriages have to last forever, and no one can *demand* that a marriage be saved. One of the worst attitudes a clergyman or any other marriage counselor—or lawmaker—can take is that something *must* be done to repair a breaking marriage. One who takes this attitude is likely to skirt the real issues. This is true also of relatives and friends who may feel that they have an obligation to keep a marriage from foundering, thus missing the entire point of the problems involved, losing them in the desire to get a couple back together even though separation or divorce may be the best solution.

Divorce, even after marriage counseling, was the right course for Mr. and Mrs. R., who came to me after eight years of marriage in which there had been no children. The first four or five years had been satisfactory for the most part; they had a good sexual relationship and enjoyed the same pastimes and had the same goals. The marriage began to sag when Mr. R. started to become a business success. Their sex life began to deteriorate and they became interested in different things—he in activities connected with business and she in civic affairs. In other words, his identity changed—he now was his *job*— and hers changed with his. They still liked each other, but the quality we describe as love did not seem to be there. They both began to engage in extramarital sex.

Here again, immaturity was evident, sexually and in other ways. Mr. R. did not provide sufficient funds for his wife, even though his earnings were quite large. She, in turn, demanded to be taken care of by him, reverting to the identity of a child. It became increasingly apparent that she wanted him around only so he would take care of her; there was no longer a desire to share mutual goals. He wanted her around to keep his illusion that he was a married man fulfilling his obligations.

These two people continued to *like* each other, but staying together would only have fed the fantasies they cherished about their marriage. Their chances of maturing would have improved if she had gone out and earned her own living and if he had been able to see marriage as something more than a set of obligations. It was clear they were not going to solve their personal problems within the context of marriage, so their best hope seemed to lie in separation.

Couples may continue to live legally under the same roof for religious or business reasons, or for the sake of their children, but in saying "I can't" or "I won't" meet the other one at least halfway, they no longer have a marriage.

Since marriage is a state in which a person's concept of himself constantly affects his relationship with his spouse, an adequate concept of personal identity is vital to a happy, growing union. The person who has some certainty of his own worth, his talents, capabilities, faults, and good points will be a marriage *partner* in the true sense of the word, able to share a mutuality of respect and understanding. Ideally, both partners in a marriage should grow, and the marriage should grow with them.

6

Lost in a Haze of Alcohol

A growing and difficult aspect of the identity crisis is the ever-rising number of drinkers, who, whether they know it or not, hope to uncork the secret of who they are every time they open a bottle. Many are steadily losing their battles to find themselves; they revert to a state of infantilism when they take hold of the bottle to nurse their disappointments, frustrations, and loneliness. It is these people in particular who either have lost their identities or never had them.

At least 9,500,000 Americans—and perhaps many more—are either problem drinkers or alcoholics, and more than 20 percent of their children will follow in their staggered footsteps. Of the nearly 10,000,000 dedicated elbow-benders, slightly more than half are alcoholics, ranging from the habitual drinker who can still hold his liquor well enough to get by with it, at least for now, to the filthy wino lolling in a Bowery doorway clutching a pint of cheap muscatel.

Every one of these people is a human being with rights and feelings—and regrets and guilt—yet there comes a time when we who are confronted by their drunken behavior get so fed up with it that we either wash our hands of them or decide we must try to "save" them. Either attitude may be justified, but there is also the possibility that neither is called for. Perhaps merely gaining an understanding of these lost souls is enough, for with understanding we may make survival, and even rehabilitation, easier for them—and for ourselves.

The haze that engulfs the alcoholic also befogs the entire subject of alcoholism itself. Even the size and scope of the problem are not entirely clear. Undoubtedly the total alcohol problem can be expressed in a much higher figure than the "educated guess" of 9,500,000 made by some experts, for there are countless "hidden alcoholics" among the men who manage to carry large quantities of liquor without presenting any overt problems as yet—and more particularly among the untold numbers of women suffering from "the housewife's secret illness," solitary drinking. Aided by their families, the women drinkers are so successful in hiding this affliction that they seldom appear in statistics. Thus, according to some sources, there may be as many as nine "hidden" men and women alcoholics for every one that is known to exist.

Alcoholism is a critical social problem, no matter how the statistics are computed. It is a problem whose components consist of the mass of all the individual problems that have made people into problem drinkers.

All of us doubtless know people who could be classified as problem drinkers or alcoholics. Some of these poor souls are members of our own families. Even the untouchable bum acquired his problem in trying to cope with life. Their problems in turn have become our problems, in one way or another. Yet it is difficult if not impossible for us to help them unless they can be motivated to want to help themselves. Until that time comes, the damage can be great psychologically, socially, and financially for all who are caught up in the tumultuous life of the problem drinker.

How can you tell when a person has become an alcoholic? Merely getting drunk, or even getting drunk with some frequency, is not necessarily a sign of a chronic problem. Only the most puritanical among us believe that having a drink means the onset of habitual intoxication. While there is no general agreement on an exact definition of alcoholism, various professional people who come into daily contact with drinkers have developed their own ideas. Dr. Laurence A. Senseman, a Lincoln, Rhode Island, physician and a leading authority on the subject, says that in essence an alcoholic is any person who has depended on alcohol to meet the ordinary demands of his daily life and who continues to drink even after his habit has caused him marital or occupational difficulty. Senseman believes that you do not have to drink every day, to drink alone, or to drink hard liquor to be an alcoholic. It is the results of the drinking, whenever it may take place, that separate the social drinkers from the drunks, he says.

The Expert Committee on Mental Health of the World Health Organization gives this definition:

"Alcoholics are those excessive drinkers whose dependence on alcohol has attained such a degree that it shows in a noticeable mental disturbance or an interference with their bodily and mental health, interpersonal relations, and their smooth social and economic functioning."

The late Dr. Robert V. Seliger of the Neuropsychiatric Hygienic Institute of Baltimore developed a list of thirty-nine questions to test whether a person was a problem drinker. He concluded that only six affirmative answers were necessary to indicate alcoholism. Here is his list:

1. Do you need a drink at a definite time every day?
2. Do you prefer drinking alone?
3. Do you find yourself getting drunk every time you drink?
4. When you drink, do you have loss of memory or blackouts?
5. Do you have the shakes after drinking?
6. Do you get the inner shakes unless you continue drinking?
7. Do you sneak your drink?
8. Do you have weekend drunks?
9. Do you have midweek drunks?
10. Do you crave a drink in the morning?
11. Do you hide your drink or protect your supply?
12. Do you desire food while drinking?
13. Do you lose time from work while drinking?
14. Has your initiative, ambition, or perseverance decreased?
15. Has drinking made you care less for your family's welfare?
16. Do you turn to an inferior environment while drinking?
17. Do you show marked moodiness while drinking?

18. Is it jeopardizing your job, business, or career?
19. Has it made you irritable or belligerent?
20. Have you ever admitted to yourself or to another that you were unable to control your drinking?
21. Has your drinking made you sensitive?
22. Do you become argumentative while drinking?
23. Is it endangering your health?
24. Is it making your home life unhappy?
25. When drinking, do you awaken early in the morning?
26. When drinking, are you restless in your sleep?
27. Do you drink to relieve feelings of inadequacy?
28. Has drinking made you harder to get along with?
29. Have you ever felt a religious need?
30. While drinking have you become extravagant in behavior?
31. Has your drinking pattern changed?
32. Do you ever have a feeling of remorse while drinking?
33. Do you engage in any antisocial behavior?
34. Do you become jealous of your husband or wife?
35. Is drinking affecting your peace of mind?
36. Have you lost any friends as a result of drinking?
37. Have you lost any jobs as a result of drinking?
38. Do you continuously seek occasions for drinking?
39. Has your life become alcohol-centered?

While a person might question the validity of some of these determinants, the questions tell us that we should not make snap judgments about an individual's drinking habits; yet, at the same time, we *can* judge from these rather clear symptoms whether we—or others—tend to have a problem in this area.

Whatever the definition, the most severe cases of alcoholism are painfully obvious. Alcoholism is one of the most trying problems a family can be forced to contend with; it amazes me when I see the naive level at which most people make an effort to deal with it. Although it is an extremely complex condition —often too complex for even a doctor or a psychiatrist to handle—people are still more likely to try to deal with alcoholism than with almost any other kind of problem.

Have you ever stopped to ask yourself why you either want or try to help an alcoholic? Has it ever occurred to you that your concern may rise out of your own feelings of guilt? It may be that when you encounter a problem drinker you are faced with your own identity quandaries, your own fears of becoming a drunk.

In any relationship with an alcoholic, keep in mind that the causes of his disease are not clear or completely known. Although there seems to be a combination of physical and psychological factors, no one has as yet come up with a definitive answer. Some say that alcoholism is a symptom of a personality or character disturbance. Others regard it as strictly an organic imbalance or the result of some other physical problem. Regardless of the cause, the alcoholic cannot control his drinking until and unless *he* musters the strength to deal with it. Therefore, to cajole him, reason with him, or preach to him is pointless, because he simply cannot help himself. Nagging is a sure invitation for an alcoholic to take another drink.

As a clergyman, I have given considerable attention to the religious implications of drinking as they pertain to the identity crisis. I began by asking this basic question: What is there in the life of the alcoholic that we can relate to religious principles? This led me straight to the obvious lack of purpose that is often felt by the alcoholic; the feeling of hopelessness he seems to carry with him as though it was his skin.

Clearly, alcoholics are not the only people who lack purpose or who are groping for identity. We have already seen that a lot of people in our society have little or no purpose, and certainly all of these do not take to drink; they express their discouragement in other ways. As can be the case with the homosexual or the narcotics addict, the alcoholic loses his sense of belonging, if, indeed, he ever really had one. He feels inferior and often inadequate, although he may not seem so to others, and he has no genuine self-respect. There appears to be a paradox in his attitudes at this point because he also feels overendowed with self-love—a rather infantile kind of self-love; a conflict develops when this feeling is not accompanied by self-respect. At this point, the alcoholic becomes anxiety-ridden; he finds himself isolated from society, and ultimately his self-love turns to self-hate. Drinking becomes his answer.

Exactly what does religion say about this? Basic in the concept of religion as we understand it is the fact of love, which may be the answer to much of the human dilemma. Christianity, for example, does not present life as hopeless or pointless or a rotten existence. Its main theme is hope and purpose, with the hope in Christianity being borne out in God's love.

The apparent paradox of self-love and self-respect becomes more easily explained when considered in a religious context. When a person has a concept of God, he becomes aware of his own limitations and he is inclined to accept them. Religion tends to keep the individual from worshiping himself. Another aspect of God's love is the worth of the human being in the context of religion, which regards every person as worth a great deal. A *truly* religious person has self-respect and yet is not guilty of having too much infantile self-love. Naturally, religion has much to say about guilt feelings, particularly when such feelings are justified. We know that the alcoholic is often ridden with justified guilt feelings stemming from his awareness that his drinking has hurt others.

To say that a man is created in the likeness or image of God is to place his life value on a high plane. This, I think, applies to the person who wants to help the alcoholic as well as to the alcoholic himself. Unless he is too weak to have faith in himself, religion can provide the alcoholic with a chance to have faith in a higher power.

This is one of the cornerstones of the success of Alcoholics Anonymous. Its founders saw the need and desire for religious principles in the life of the alcoholic. A member may proceed with or without a religious objective, with or without any affiliation with organized religion, but the fact remains that these principles exist in the famous "twelve steps" of A.A. For example, a member is required to acknowledge he is powerless over alcohol. One of the steps speaks also of dependence on a "higher power" and another of confession and restitution. These are largely ethical considerations that are often seen in the context of religious thought, and they have been used effectively by A.A.

Identity—or the lack of it—enters the A.A. program in another way. A member of A.A. does not call himself a *former* alcoholic. He does not say he has been *cured*. He says, *"I am an alcoholic who does not drink."* In the identity structure, he still wears the face of an alcoholic, but he now knows it, accepts it, and admits it to others. In short, he does not lie to himself.

The best and most effective work in saving alcoholics has been accomplished by A.A.'s ability to offer a supportive approach. It is actually a form of group therapy, providing a Big Brother to lean on, someone who will help another in a crisis, someone who has "been there" himself. This gives a clue to what goes on within the alcoholic, apart from the organic or chemical activity. Dynamically what he feels inside is a tremendous deprivation, usually suffered at a very early age. In a very real psychological sense this person was not fulfilled somewhere along the line, emotionally or materially.

When an alcoholic goes on a binge, he is expressing a need either to be overwhelmingly dependent or to escape reality. He blocks out the world. In a way, he goes into retreat. I know a woman alcoholic, for instance, who literally goes into hiding during periodic drinking bouts. She goes to bed, alone, with a bottle and drinks herself into infantile oblivion.

Another woman alcoholic admitted her childishness by saying: "I am emotionally immature. My parents have helped me too much. They are still helping me. They paid for plane fare when I left my husband and for my divorce, too. I was the kind who took a drink at home before I went to a cocktail party. I needed Dutch courage. My husband did not know about my drinking, but he found out. That ended everything for us."

This woman was able to talk this way only after she had been "dried out" and started her life anew. She accepted counseling when her husband divorced her, taking their children with him. She was helped only because she *wanted* help. Motivating the alcoholic to take this course is very difficult, and it often takes a catastrophe such as divorce to jolt one into action.

Occasionally—very occasionally—alcoholics seek professional counseling. One of the principal problems in trying to help them is the difficulty in getting them to remain sober long enough to *be* helped. I find that I can reach an alcoholic only if he remains dry, at least during the actual counseling sessions, and so I will generally not keep an appointment when a client comes in inebriated. Since much of counseling and psychotherapy requires the use of reason in achieving an understanding of feelings, particularly feelings that get out of control under the influence of alcohol, it is usually hopeless to try to reach a person who is drunk. My decision generally not to see a person "under the influence" has no bearing on his worth but rather on the need to adhere to certain conditions in the counseling relationship.

Members of families of alcoholics must often set limits— the point beyond which they will not tolerate the presence of the family inebriate. A wife, for example, must decide how long she will put up with a sodden husband. She also should look deep into her own person to try to discover if she is aggravating the drinking problem by nagging about it, or at the other extreme, by pretending it does not exist. A husband or wife who ignores the fact that a spouse is alcoholic often encourages the illness by denying it.

For example, if a woman says, "I don't care to go further with this. I realize my husband is sick but I cannot tolerate any more," she may be behaving quite reasonably. But if she says, "I do not care to go further with this because my husband is a disgrace and unworthy," perhaps *she* has a problem, too.

In most cases, it requires years for alcoholism to take its toll of an individual, physically, mentally, emotionally, economically, and in other ways. He may function reasonably well for several decades before he falls apart. Male alcoholics tend to hit the peak of their daily intake in their most productive years, after having devoted a decade or two to becoming full-blown drunks. Perhaps some pressing problem in his early years has left a man psychologically damaged. Or he may have been unable to develop the part of his personality that keeps the need for gratification under control, the thermostat that puts a rein on the desire for one more "very dry Martini on the rocks, with a twist, please." Sometimes, of course, this control works the other way, becoming so overactive that a person is so rigid that he deprives himself of *all* pleasure. This also involves an identity problem that will be dealt with in the next chapter.

As far as the alcoholic is concerned, we should give particular heed to the psychological aspects of drinking in order to understand not only something of what he experiences when he is gripped by an anxiety with which he is unable to cope, but what the family of the alcoholic experiences as it is faced with the fantastically complex involvements that confront the drinker, in terms of both psychological strain and such practical difficulties as handling money, functioning on the job, running afoul of the law, etc.

Two stories, one about a man, the other a woman, may help to clarify the problem. He started drinking in his teens and was "hooked" by the time he reached middle age, while she drank to build defenses against periodic crises in her life.

A. K. came for counseling when he was fifty-six years old, with a history of drinking that began with cheap wine at the age of fifteen. He was married at twenty and managed to complete college and a few graduate courses before the first of his three children was born. A physically strong man despite his lifelong bout with the bottle, he had tried A.A. periodically for nearly twenty years but still could not remain sober for more than a few weeks at a stretch.

Despite his drinking, A. K. had held several responsible positions in industry. However, every time he was about to reach the top, the taste of success became too much for him to bear, and he managed to become embroiled in a drinking spree that would cause him either to be fired or to run away on a prolonged juvenile escapade.

When he came in, desperate for help, after many years of drinking, he still did not display many outward signs of emotional or intellectual deterioration. But as his story unfolded, it became obvious that he was seething with anxiety just below the surface. When sober he usually could keep his fright under a degree of control, but only up to a point. When he could stand the torment no longer, he got drunk, sometimes staying that way for weeks. He took flight physically as well, usually running off to another part of the country for his binges. In his sober periods, once he formed an opinion, he seldom would change it or even consider another aspect of a situation. This rigidity often was his last defense; it kept him under control on many occasions, but sometimes it also became too much for him to bear, so he went out and got drunk.

Running away, emotionally, psychologically, and physically, was the solution to any situation too anxiety-producing for A. K. He never had the strength within himself to stay and face the facts. So unsure of himself did he become that he had to present a forceful exterior; he *had* to feel he was always right, a trait that in most people tends to indicate a high degree of insecurity. He was no exception.

A. K. did not last long in treatment. He was not able to face the facts of his own life, and eventually when he became involved in a serious family quarrel, he succumbed again. He ran away on another drunken escapade and I never saw him again.

The woman alcoholic, whom we shall call Priscilla, presents a different sort of story, and a more hopeful one. She sought help at the age of forty-four after sixteen years of drinking. During the first twenty-eight years of her life alcohol had presented no problem. As a professional woman she had been able to be a social drinker—until a crisis confronted her. While in her late twenties and early thirties she became involved in a marital situation that was more than she could bear and that she did not know how to handle. She was married to a man who was not able to share a sexual relationship with her, who had to use her for his own psychological needs. This became a terrible strain on her. Instead of leaving him, however, she kept hoping for fulfillment because she loved him. Her escape from this situation was drinking. Ironically, it was he who got the divorce.

Priscilla displayed a marked lack of a sense of identity (as did her husband), but there was a major difference between her subsequent attitudes and those of A. K. In the course of therapy, she had the will and motivation to sustain herself in times of tremendous anxiety without having to escape to the bottle or run away from herself in any other sense of the word. Both she and A. K. had sought escape in drinking when their anxieties built to a point where they could not handle them. However, she had much more strength than he, and she has made a new start in life as an "alcoholic who does not drink."

How do members of the family deal with the A.K.s and Priscillas of the world?

First, by minimizing demands for them to do "something." Too many people feel compelled to cure or help an alcoholic, which is a frustrating effort in most cases because alcoholics, as we have seen, are often poorly motivated to stop drinking and tend to deny even to themselves that they need to stop. Hope is in sight only at the moment they recognize what their trouble is.

Second, relatives are often embarrassed at having an alcoholic in the family; they feel it is a reflection on *them.* True, it can be quite inconvenient when a father gets into trouble on his job, or a husband becomes sloppy drunk and is arrested for speeding. But this does not mean that the nondrinking member of the family is superior as a person and the alcoholic is inferior, even though he has a problem that may make him seem so.

Third, the family must realize that it is not responsible for a person's becoming an alcoholic. If you have a brother who has a drinking problem, you might offer to help him, but you do not have to, nor are you expected to go the entire route with him. The alcoholism certainly is not your fault. If you feel guilty about it, that is *your* problem.

Here again is where A.A. can help the alcoholic more effectively than can the family. A.A. provides these three basic aids, which so far as I know are not available in most other environments:

1. A completely unjudgmental atmosphere but yet one that insists a person must take responsibility for his own actions.

2. A great deal of support by other members of A.A. who have been faced with a similar problem.

3. A policy of placing an obligation on the alcoholic to do something about his problem, something active, even at times creative. It also expects him to do something in terms of making amends—restitution—where wrongs have been done, and to refrain from minimizing or denying the fact that he has a problem.

Ideally, the substitution of other activities for drinking could be helpful to the alcoholic. Because A.A. does this effectively, however, does not mean that you will accomplish the same end by saying to your neighbor, "Say, Joe, instead of drinking all day, why don't you go bowling or make a swing for the kids to play on or something like that?" This is likely to have as little effect as any other kind of cajoling. It can be too condescending. At the same time, we have to be careful to avoid even so much as a hint that we regard everyone with a drinking problem as a candidate for skid row. Some of the most literate, creative, and worthwhile members of our society—when they are able to function—have drinking problems.

The family of the habitual tippler, whether it be Mother sneaking the sherry or Dad pulling a pint of bourbon out of a golf bag, usually is the least able to help because it is too close to the problem. Also, the family itself may have suffered severely at the hands of the alcoholic in reaction to their carping or some other irritating practice such as pouring the liquor supply down the sink.

Even the outsider, professional or otherwise, who offers to help the alcoholic is taking on a very difficult assignment. He is making himself available for calls at all hours of the day and night and under the most trying circumstances. Moreover, he is assuming a great responsibility to the person. If for some reason the alcoholic's demands cannot be met at a specific time, he feels he has been let down. Consequently, any offer to help a drinker is one that is not to be made lightly. The rehabilitated drinker can be the most helpful, for he is willing to devote the time and effort that the rest of us may not be able or want to offer. As in A.A., the "dried-out" alcoholic can speak the language of the drunk going through delirium tremens, and herein often lies a tremendous amount of supportive help.

While professional assistance or the sympathetic support of another alcoholic seems most appropriate, there are several ways friends and relatives can be helpful, largely by *not* doing anything, but also by taking firm steps when necessary. Here are a few words of advice:

• Accept alcoholism as an illness with psychological and physical components. Face it just as you would any other illness. Understanding and support are the best help you can provide.

• Don't feel it is your obligation to keep on bearing the brunt of the abuses that alcoholics can inflict. Draw a line beyond which you will not go. Once a decision is made, stick to it. Spouses of alcoholics often make threats they do not carry out. Threats do not make alcoholics "shape up." Their problem has nothing to do with the exercise of will power, and this is what you appeal to with an empty threat. Before deciding on an action or an ultimatum, think it through carefully, trying to consider all of its ramifications. Then ask yourself if this is what you really intend to do. Make it a decision rather than a threat.

• Don't moralize or lecture or cajole the alcoholic. It will not help the situation and it might make it worse.

A friend or other outsider can learn to cope with the alcoholic, without trying to effect a cure, by understanding as much as possible about what alcoholism is, what may cause it, and how alcoholics react. Perhaps it would be desirable to try to guide the drinker to A.A. or some other supportive environment where he can get treatment. While there are some alcoholic personalities that do not fit into the A.A. program, many of them seem to get reasonably well and manage to sustain themselves in the organization.

There is another kind of help the outsider can provide: assistance for the long-suffering and often deprived family of the drinker. You can help them become acquainted with the available facts about alcoholism and give them the kind of moral support they need, first by bringing them to the realization that having a drinker in the family is not a reflection on them and that they will not be rejected by society because of it; and, second, by encouraging them to understand that if they cannot help or cure the family alcoholic, it does not mean they have failed.

The samaritan sometimes can provide the greatest assistance by helping to ease the financial and other burdens the presence of an alcoholic wage-earner can create. Helping a wife find a job often releases some of the tension and worry; I have seen cases where the sight of a wife going off to work in the morning has encouraged a husband to make an earnest effort to stop drinking.

If none of these things is done, just being a patient listener can often relieve the strain on the family of the alcoholic. Mere knowledge that someone is interested in their welfare can bring comfort.

It should be emphasized that many alcoholics have a great feeling, even love, for their families; their damaging behavior is something they cannot help and deeply regret. Remorse is one of the major emotions of the alcoholic going through the pangs of a hangover. Not for one moment should we think that the alcoholic really enjoys drinking; what is a nightmare and tragedy for his family, friends, and business associates is a double nightmare for him. His wife and children will spare themselves much grief if they become aware of this. They also should be warned to accept the fact that there is no perfect cure and not be too discouraged by relapses. Above all, the family must be led to understand that it does not help to argue with an alcoholic, to cover up his transgressions, or to treat him as an irresponsible child.

How much must a family put up with if the alcoholic refuses treatment? What should be done with him as he continues to deteriorate? Should he be institutionalized? Is divorce or separation the answer? There are no clear-cut answers to these questions, but there are times after all else has failed when institutionalization or divorce is necessary. Neither step solves the alcoholic's problem unless he is jolted into action as was Priscilla when her husband walked out on her in disgust, taking the children with him, but it can save the rest of the family from continued misery.

One of the most unfortunate aspects of drinking is that the children of alcoholics are more likely than the children of non-drinkers to have the same kind of identity problems that led to the bottle. A study made some years ago showed that 20 to 30 percent of the children of alcoholics were likely to become heavy drinkers, while the probability among the population as a whole was 2 percent. Such a finding raises a question whether there are inherited physical characteristics that provide a predisposition for alcohol or whether the illness is produced environmentally.

There are psychological ramifications, of course, since the child who sees his parents trying to solve their problems with liquor may conclude that this is an accepted way to escape from reality. I recall a man who said to me not long after he had sobered up from a three-day spree: "How could I be any different after watching my father get drunk every time he had a problem while I was growing up? I grew up thinking this was the only way out of a tough spot, so that's the system I have used to handle my difficulties." This fellow was about as lost as anyone I have ever encountered, for he was identifying himself with a father who, throughout his lifetime, did not know who *he* was either.

There are, of course, offspring of alcoholics who take the opposite route and refrain from touching a drop. They often are rigid in other ways and have as much difficulty finding their identities as those who take the alcoholic path. I'll never forget Daniel the night he created a scene in a restaurant by knocking some drinks off the table, losing three friends with that one gesture.

7

Jellyfish in Armor

Daniel really thought he was a "good guy," but actually he did not have the remotest idea how to go about relaxing and enjoying himself. He clung to the notion that having fun and getting drunk were synonymous, and as the son of an alcoholic, he had become so extremely rigid about liquor that he would rather not think about having a good time. To him one drink was one too many, not just for him but for anyone, and he extended his rigid attitude into other phases of his life.

For example, Daniel became a bookkeeper. He liked the discipline of numbers. For twenty years he had held the same job, reporting for work at the same time every day, going to lunch at almost exactly the stroke of noon and never failing to catch the five-fifteen for home and dinner at six P.M. "sharp." He allowed himself to sleep one extra hour on Saturday and Sunday mornings, not a minute more or less, and he ate exactly the same breakfast every day. When it came time for a vacation, every summer Daniel took his wife and children to the same seaside resort during the month of August. He always wore white shirts, pale ties, and green socks. Although he had several suits, they were all brown and of exactly the same style and material. In bad weather he not only wore rubbers and a raincoat but fitted a plastic covering over his hat and carried an umbrella. He also carried a coin purse instead of allowing coins to fall loosely in his pocket as most men do.

Daniel's identity problem was wrapped up in the fact that the last person he wanted to resemble was his father, a harddrinking, free-spending ne'er-do-well. In fact he devoted so much time to trying not to be his father that he never allowed himself to become *himself*. Under his armor, he was a jellyfish, but he made everyone think he was a pillar of strength.

Overcontrol had become as much of a habit with Daniel as the apparent lack of will power had been with his father. It was a matter of self-denial as opposed to self-indulgence. While Daniel did not become the social problem his father had been, he certainly did not give himself a chance to enjoy the social amenities of life, and he made his wife and children downright miserable at times.

Daniel was a bright, often pleasant man and seemed to get along reasonably well until he saw anyone he knew take a drink or heard one word about liquor. He would become so upset that he would launch into a lecture on the evils of drink. This behavior began when Daniel was a teen-ager, but it became more pronounced as he grew older. He joined prohibitionist organizations and supported their candidates for political office. He attended a church whose minister shared his views on temperance, and he took great pains not to even listen to anyone else's ideas on the subject.

As you can imagine, a person this rigid would not have many friends. Most of Daniel's acquaintances were people he had known as a boy who accepted his "eccentricities" as he grew up. But he lost even the oldest and best of these old friends the night he created a scene in a restaurant.

Daniel and his wife were dining with his old friend Bob and his wife. They had not seen one another for several years, and when Bob came to town, he invited Daniel and his wife to dinner. When Bob and his wife ordered cocktails, Daniel made a few rather cutting remarks, and by the time the drinks arrived, he had worked up a head of steam. No sooner had the waiter set the drinks down than Daniel, with one sweeping gesture of his right hand, knocked both of them over, sending streams of liquor into the laps of his host and hostess.

Bob and his wife were furious and soon departed. The proprietor of the restaurant, a usually genial man who had helped Daniel's reeling father out of the establishment on many an evening, was embarrassed to the point of anger. Since the community in which this incident occurred was small, word of this latter-day male version of Carrie Nation swept through town, and Daniel was the laughing stock of many a dinner-table conversation for several days.

When he was informed that he had made a fool of himself, Daniel characteristically replied that he did not care. *He* knew what was right and he had acted accordingly. Everyone else was out of step as far as he was concerned. What he did not realize was that because he could not trust himself to take so much as a sniff or a sip of liquor, he never would be able to trust anyone else to do so either. I do not know whether he ever became aware of this truth about himself, but I doubt it. The Daniels seem to go through life imposing their ideas on people and trying to impose their wills as well, without ever really knowing who they themselves are or fulfilling a very meaningful role within their own family circles.

In Daniel's case, he drove his children from home earlier than they might have left had he been a more tolerant, flexible person. They drank at the homes of their friends and went off to college, where they consumed more than their share of alcohol. Neither developed into a problem drinker, but they never forgave their father for his rigidity. Ultimately he spent many lonely evenings wondering why other people his age received visits from their children while his rarely came to see him.

Such strong views on alcohol provide only one facet of the rigid personality. Racial and religious bigotry are symptoms of rigidity and, in the final analysis, of a deep identity quandary. People who are secure in their self-knowledge seldom find themselves threatened by members of other races and religions. The bigot, being insecure, and even afraid, although his outward appearance may belie this state, feels threatened or he would not react so strongly to those who are different from him to any great degree.

I encounter quite a bit of religious rigidity among members of the clergy. Unfortunately, a good many men turn to the pulpit because of their rigidities, rationalizing their views by thinking that they are expected of one who wears the cloth. Harold was one of these ministers. When he spoke from the pulpit, he produced a crescendo of stentorian tones about hellfire and damnation. There were those in the congregation who liked it when he sounded like a modern-day Moses standing before the people laying down the "moral law" of the land; it made them feel more comfortable to listen to a voice of authority booming down on them in their pews.

But to others, Harold was a source of discomfort, annoyance, and outright dislike. Those who cringed as he cried out were disturbed by the tone of finality in his "direct quotations" from the Almighty. These were bad enough when he dealt with matters theological, but when he got down to everyday subjects, it was even more grating. Harold disagreed sharply with the more liberal interpretations of others, and when he argued with them, he tended to do so in venomous and even violently judgmental tones. Ultimately he reached the point where he could not—and would not—examine any theological or social idea that did not correspond with his own position.

His rigidity finally created a crisis at a weekly meeting of the governing board of his church. Several young people had asked for permission to hold a dance in the parish house, something that never had been done during Harold's tenure as minister. He had made it clear that he did not favor the idea, but the young people decided to make a formal request anyway. Several board members took the moderate view that social activities for young people at the church would be wholesome. They felt that it would be good for the entire community if the church became a center that attracted youngsters.

It was apparent to all at the meeting that Harold began bristling the moment the subject was broached. The discussion rapidly became heated, so much so that his patience obviously wore thin. The fact that he was in a minority made matters worse. Finally, no longer able to contain himself, he blurted:

"What do you think will happen if we permit such a function in our church? What will happen to boys and girls dancing with their bodies close to each other? I'll tell you what will happen. The next thing you know they'll all be out in their cars and half the girls will end up pregnant!"

Further, Harold declared that if a dance was permitted in the parish house, he would make a public issue of it from the pulpit and resign from the church. Knowing the difficulty of finding a new minister for a small town and aware of Harold's diligence at church tasks and devotion to calling on the sick and the aged, the board relented and decided not to create a public crisis over this event. Word of the minister's rigidity reached the young people, however, and slowly most of them left the church. So did three of the most active and generous adult supporters of the congregation. Harold did not care; after all, *he* was right! The sinners had gone elsewhere!

In actuality, Harold, without knowing it, was making an interesting public confession in his unbending opposition to dancing. What he was saying was that he did not trust *himself* under the conditions that prevail on a dance floor, and therefore no one else could be trusted either. He was saying that he was so bound by his own rigidity that he expected the whole world to be like him. He also was expressing his insecurity, his fear of examining another position.

There is another kind of rigidity worth mentioning here— the individual who is "right" no matter what the evidence may be. As an example of this kind of inflexibility, let me tell you about Sarah M., whose son was tried for murder. The evidence against the young man was quite overwhelming, or at least the jury thought so, for it convicted him of second-degree murder. Sarah refused to accept the verdict, insisting that her son was the victim of a "frame-up," in which the body of his best girl was planted in his automobile on a lonely lover's lane. She had no explanation for the fact that he was found wandering incoherently in the night a short distance away, with a piece of the girl's torn clothing in his hand.

Because the case was of considerable interest in the community, several investigations were conducted, but no evidence was ever turned up to warrant a verdict other than the one the jury had reached in fourteen hours of deliberation.

Sarah held fast to her belief in her son's innocence. When I asked her why she kept pressing for new investigations to exonerate him, she replied that it was purely in the interest of justice and out of a desire to "find the truth." I then asked whether she would really want to find the truth if it proved without doubt that her son was guilty.

"Of course," she replied, "but I know that if such an investigation is honestly conducted, it will prove his innocence!"

Again I asked how she would react if the evidence proved otherwise, and again she responded: "That is just not possible because *I* know he is innocent!"

Still another rigid view of the world stems from being injected into a competitive situation that can become a threat to one's concept of himself. The best way I can illustrate this is to tell you about a group of men I observed some years ago when I was working in a psychiatric hospital. It was customary for members of the staff to meet periodically for conferences on some of the patients. I recall that on one occasion

three ward doctors were sitting side by side during a conference. After all the data had been presented, the meeting was
open for a discussion of the case. One of the three stood up
and made several remarks prefaced by: "Now, this is what is
going on with the patient, and this is what should be done."
The two others got up in turn and began in substantially the
same way. Yet each gave a different diagnosis and plan of
treatment, and each did this without reacting in any way to
what the others had said.

When the psychiatrist in charge of the conference pointed
out their differences of opinion, the three fell into a heated
discussion, with each declaring that *his* observations were the
only ones with any validity, and all refusing even to consider
differing views.

Subsequently I learned that these three men had known one
another for many years. They had received their training at
the same school and had always been in keen competition.
Each was working on a pet theory about mental illness and
turned deaf ears to the ideas of the others. Their competitive
feelings were such that each saw the others as threats to his
career. All had narrow, rigid views of the professional world in
which they worked and poor senses of who they were—at least
while they were on duty.

Despite the fact that the three were scientists, they were
caught up in the kind of identity crises that they dealt with
every day in their work. Their reactions on a professional
level grew out of their own feelings about themselves as surely
as Daniel's attitude toward drinking was a product of his
feelings about himself. In Daniel's case he was obviously
afraid that if he was at all tolerant he might take a drink, and

that if he did, he might not be able to control the urge for another and another and another, and so on, until he was a falling-down drunk like his father.

Harold was obviously so afraid of his own sexual desires that he kept them artificially in check, repressing them with proclamations of religious fervor. He hid behind an attitude so rigid that he led people to feel that to disagree with him was to disagree with the Almighty. Actually, he did not have the courage to be himself.

In his book on *The Individual and His Religion,* Gordon Alport discusses people whose religious beliefs are so rigid that they are difficult to be with. He explains that the reason such a person cannot even listen to—let alone examine—a thought or belief that is contrary to his own is that he is afraid that if one stone of his structure of belief is removed, the whole structure will topple like a castle in the sand being washed away by a small wave.

Sarah, for example, let both her son and herself become victims of her rigidity. Years before his arrest on the murder charge, the boy had been involved in a minor scrape with the police. At that time the mother was advised to seek professional help for him, but she denied that anything could possibly be "wrong" with her boy and so she did nothing. She even became abusive toward the social worker who had the temerity to make such a suggestion. It was apparent that her later reaction to my questions was based on her unconscious reluctance to face the possibility of her son's guilt because it then would threaten her feelings about herself as a mother and perhaps also as a person.

This brings us to some basic reasons why some people assume unbending positions on various matters during their lives. We who are exposed to rigid personalities tend to become annoyed, angry, and frustrated by them. When this happens, we take the attitude that they are addressing their views solely to us. Actually they are acting out of their own need to sell us their view of the world; if the world does not "buy" it, they are upset and may even feel threatened.

The primary reason for rigidity has little to do with anyone other than the person who suffers from this social and emotional affliction. It involves mainly the inner feelings of the rigid individual—his own self-concept. Somewhere along the way, as he grew from infancy through childhood and adolescence into adulthood, his feelings about his identity either were damaged or did not develop properly. In some cases, as in that of Daniel, it is reasonably simple to see how insecurity can develop under a mask of what could be mistakenly regarded as strength but which actually is inflexibility.

In Daniel's case—and in others, too—without his being aware of it, his strongly expressed prohibitions provided him with a shell—armor to protect him from feeling fearful that he would lose control. The more pronounced the rigidity, the more likely the person may be to collapse without it. Thus while those around him may regard him as an "iron man," in actuality he is like the turtle who lives in an impenetrable fortress as long as he is encased in his shell. Take away his armor and he is defenseless and almost surely will die.

There can be any number of reasons for the development of this type of defense mechanism. Underlying each is an inadequately developed sense of one's own being. Whether in response to a need to comply with the wishes of an iron-willed parent or in reaction against a parental attitude that is distasteful, the inflexible person tends to be one who has not been able to separate himself from his own thoughts, ideas, and feelings. His concept of himself is so shaky that he is saying in effect, "Since I am my feelings and ideas, if you reject my feelings and ideas you reject *me*."

Because rigid people tend to be unpleasant companions, it is quite natural to react strongly to them. Our capacity to be tolerant of them may be strained to the breaking point. Their insecurity, combined with the strained relationships they produce, allows us to perceive quite easily their propensity for destructiveness. It is harder to find something constructive in rigidity than in indulgence. Yet we must consider that rigidity often is a kind of glue that keeps a person stuck together. Sometimes it is better to listen in silence to the sermonizing of the inflexible person than to argue and witness their collapse.

Perhaps the best way to cope with a rigid person is to develop a secure sense of one's own identity. It is almost a certainty that an argument will not change an inflexible stand. As in the case of Sarah, logic and even proof were of no avail in efforts to budge her from her belief that her son was innocent. If a person's rigidity does not affect your own freedom of action, it may be best to ignore it as much as possible—difficult though that may be. Unfortunately, rigidity cannot always be ignored, however, because inflexible people reach positions of influence and power, as was the case with the late Senator Joseph McCarthy, who did not let the truth lead him from his self-appointed task as an arbiter of public political views. It was also the case with Adolf Hitler, to take the most extreme example one can imagine. And it is the case with every bigot you encounter who makes declarations against Jews, Negroes, Italians, or any other group in our society.

To give a less serious example, I once had the unhappy experience of working with a man who was so rigid that it was unpleasant to be in the same room with him. He could not tolerate having anything done in any way except the one he thought proper. This might not have been so terrible if he had been in charge, but he was just another member of a group, so his censoriousness made for considerable tension in the department. In short, he made life unpleasant for all who worked with him. I, like others who came into daily contact with him, learned that the only way to cope with him was to ignore him; we simply withdrew from his unpleasantness. This helped us, but it caused him to become nasty and sometimes violent toward anyone who did not see things his way. Occasionally he would report to superiors when colleagues were not performing their tasks as he saw fit.

It came as no surprise to me when I learned some years later that his wife had left him after he refused to speak to her because she had done something contrary to his wishes. His son reacted to his rigidity by withdrawing from society as a "hippie." The father is a very lonely man today, and undoubtedly is wondering what is wrong with all of those who have dropped out of his life—or were pushed out.

A person as rigid as this seldom changes unless he becomes involved in a long-term therapeutic relationship or unless a situation occurs in his life that shakes the very foundations of his being.

Yet we ask ourselves how anyone could be so rigid in his

views, particularly in our so-called enlightened times of scientific evidence and proof. But the fact is that many of us manifest some kind of rigidity to some degree at some time in our lives. For example, we observe a housewife who is so enslaved to her own schedule for dusting, sweeping, washing dishes, bed-making, etc., that she will not deviate for any except the most dire emergency. The man who votes Republican or Democratic because that is the way his father and grandfather voted, or the person who must eat exactly the same things for breakfast every day is behaving quite rigidly.

I recall having breakfast once with a nurse in the throes of "breakfast rigidity" at a hospital where I worked. The menu in the staff dining room usually offered a choice of eggs or something else, but on this particular morning eggs were not available. The nurse, a stranger to me, turned and said: "That can't be! I eat two eggs every day of my life. Eggs are very good for you. I eat two eggs every day of my life. I can't start the day without my eggs!"

She chastized the waitress and turned to me again: "How can they do this?"

I listened silently as she became increasingly upset. Finally, however, she settled for coffee and toast, but not without more complaints.

While I certainly never would quarrel with the idea that eggs are good for you, I found the nurse's inflexibility completely without reason. Why, I asked myself, was she in such a rut that she became annoyed and upset when her system of eating was disrupted in such a minor way? Then I looked at my own habit patterns and had to admit that I, too, am inflexible about breakfast. I am one of the millions of coffee drinkers who *must* have my favorite beverage in the morning before I consume anything else—coffee and orange juice and *then* whatever else is being served. On several occasions, my wife has served me eggs first, suggesting I eat them before they got cold. My response? "I want my coffee and juice first!"

The breakfast ritual probably is one of our most deeply embedded social rigidities. There is no reason why one should not eat steak and pie or spaghetti and meat balls for breakfast instead of ham and eggs or the other "standard" fare. However, we cling to the so-called breakfast foods, as persistently as Linus clutches his security blanket in the Peanuts cartoon, out of our need to start the day with a feeling of security. If we deviate from our set pattern, we are likely to become anxious for unconscious reasons. It is possible for us to vary our lunch and dinner menus, and even the time we have these meals, but breakfast is often the cornerstone of our day.

Many of us have other habits that betoken varying degrees and kinds of rigidity. For example, I know a man who tries the door on his automobile three times after he has locked it; only then is he satisfied that it is secure. I have seen people habitually switch lights on and off two or three times instead of once. During a recent business meeting I watched with fascination while a colleague carefully unwrapped a stick of chewing gum and then after he had put it in his mouth just as carefully put the entire wrapper together so that it looked as though it had never been touched. He did this several times in the course of one day.

Some people will eat the food on their plates in a certain

order. A friend of mine has told me about a relative who, when he ate mashed potatoes, always meticulously flattened them to the plate with his fork, trimmed off the edges to make a square, and then consumed them in geometrically precise squares. Such people may be horrified at the dietary idiosyncrasies of others.

I also venture to guess that everyone has his own particular order of getting dressed in the morning. I do, and when for some reason I vary the system, I must admit that I become confused and tend to forget something—my handkerchief, my watch, or some other item.

Now these minor compulsive habits that we all have are not necessarily socially damaging in the way that the inflexibilities of people such as Daniel and Sarah are. There is nothing wrong with some of our persistently repetitious acts, for they help us to maintain a kind of balance. But they can limit our ability to experience life and express ourselves in creative and diversified ways—and they may be indications of identity problems.

The housewife who is so bound up in her life that she identifies herself with housekeeping can interfere with the lives of her husband and children by enslaving them to her routine, too. The husband who will not break his Saturday schedule of chores and watching football on TV has not learned to live in relation to other people and consider their wishes, because he is wrapped up in himself.

Rigidity sometimes gives people a feeling of power and thus more worth. This kind of identity-seeking is found in the executive who is invariably too busy to see a subordinate or who says, "I can spare you only five minutes," and then engages in conversation for an hour. He finds his identity in the power of being able to set the time and terms and then altering them as he sees fit.

What may seem socially harmless rigidities can still interfere with people's lives. I knew a girl who felt compelled to take three baths a day, each of long duration, rather like Blanche in *A Streetcar Named Desire*. Although you may say that this was *her* business and *her* problem, in reality it interfered with other people's lives. She was late for appointments. She monopolized the bathroom.

How about you? What are your inflexibilities? You almost surely have some. Why don't you take stock of yourself by making a list of the things you do repeatedly and habitually day after day? Do you always eat the same things for breakfast? Are you unhappy when what you want is not available *when* you want it or do you readily accept alternatives? Do you ever vary your breakfast menu or the time for having breakfast? Do you always follow the same ritual in dressing and undressing, bathing, getting ready for bed? Jot down the things you do as you go through a day and then make a note of the rigidities and inflexibilities of friends and relatives that you find annoying. Compare their habits with yours and then ask yourself whether they might not find your inflexibilities irritating at times.

Your answers will not necessarily mean that you should break any of the routines with which you have cushioned your life. They obviously make you feel more secure within yourself and in the world. But if you recognize some of these habits and have some understanding of *why* you have them, you will gain not only a better sense of your own identity but a deeper understanding and a greater acceptance of the foibles of others. You might also find yourself becoming less rigid—more flexible—and liking yourself and others better.

8

The Lonesome Strangers

We hear a lot about mental retardation these days, and millions of dollars and thousands of scientific man-hours are being devoted to this human tragedy. But there is another kind of handicap that affects millions of people and causes misery and yet is largely being ignored or treated punitively by society.

That human problem is homosexuality.

While we generally think of retardation in terms of the mongoloid, the mentally deficient, the physically deformed or crippled, it is also appropriate to regard many of the problems relating to questions of a person's identity as resulting from a kind of emotional inadequacy—"retardation," if you will. Homosexuality is one form of emotional retardation.

There is in our country a huge "invisible minority" of homosexuals or homosexually inclined men and women who, while not suffering from birth defects, are handicapped because of events in their childhood that have caused them to deviate from the normal pattern of sexual development. The exact number of those so affected is not known, of course, but it has been estimated that there are as many as seventeen million practicing homosexuals, with possibly 10 percent of the entire male population—ten million—having been exclusively homosexual for at least three years of their lives. The late Dr. Alfred C. Kinsey made studies that indicated that about 50 percent of all American males have some homosexual "response," although somewhat less—about one third—have actually engaged in overt homosexual practices. By the age of sixteen, it appears, 90 percent of all males have settled on the sexual preference that will dominate their lives.

What does this tell us? It tells us that a staggering number of men and women are confused—at least to some degree—as to their sexual identity. In many instances, they express this confusion without even being aware of their dilemma. It tells us also that to turn our back on the homosexual problem, the homosexual situation, or the homosexual person is to turn our back on a rather common problem involving human development—or the lack of it. It may mean that we are closing our eyes to the problems of people close to us. And since sexual identity is so fundamental to emotional development, it may mean we are turning our backs on our own best interests.

Mental retardation has been a subject openly discussed only in the last few years. Parents now acknowledge they have defective children, whereas in times not so long past, the "village idiot" was held up to scorn, or a family locked its mongoloid child in a room where it remained throughout its life. Mental illness, too, has become a publicly discussed handicap and is being battled on many fronts. Although there is now much more discussion about the homosexual and wider acceptance of his activities, he often remains scorned and even vilified in many areas of our society. The practice of homosexuality is outlawed in every state except Illinois, where consenting adults are allowed to fraternize in private without interference. The laws in the other states define homosexual acts in various ways, principally as sodomy. They level a variety of charges and mete out punishments ranging from slight to severe. It has been said that 95 percent of the adult males in this country have at some time in their lives violated one or more laws regulating sexual activities—heterosexual as well as homosexual. Because the laws are unenforceable, punishment has been relatively infrequent.

With homosexuality still thus stigmatized, it may come as a surprise to many to learn that some everyday activities and attitudes have the overtones of the kind of homosexual feelings that are widely condemned. This is understandable when we think of the way a person develops sexually. In the normal course of development all of us go through a stage in which we prefer the company of members of our own sex. The activities we engage in later in our lives that tend to exclude members of the opposite sex are residues of this period. Yet some people may be discomfited to learn that the women's bridge club, the exclusive men's club, and even certain sports activities have, in the broadest sense, overtones of homosexuality. Their existence certainly indicates a desire for the company of one's own sex to the exclusion of the other, at least part of the time. As such, they are a residue of that period of development before puberty when boys prefer to be with boys and girls seek out girls for playmates. To put it more bluntly, they are a residue of the homosexual period of development.

All of us know at least one Don Juan (he has his female counterpart, too), who appears to want to seduce every attractive woman he sees and who spends a lot of time boring others with elaborate stories of his sexual triumphs. There is a homosexual component in this man, for he is usually in the throes of a sexual identity crisis in which he hopes to reassure himself of his masculinity even more than he hopes to impress his audience. Like the kid in school who brags about his exploits, the Don Juan thrives on boasting. Do not be confused by the man who expounds on his sexual prowess. Do not be too impressed, either, for he probably is merely seeking some kind of assurance that he really is a man.

At the other extreme, we find the person who indicates his doubts about his own sexual identity by taking a rigidly strong and censorious view of homosexuals. The person who is secure in himself as an individual is secure about himself sexually and, therefore, is able to accept a homosexual as another person on the same terms that he is able to accept a person who is physically ill or handicapped.

However, because of a lack of understanding of their circumstances and also because some overt homosexuals tend to be such caricatures of the opposite sex, nearly all homosexuals are forced into a hidden minority haunted by fear, rejected by society and the church, and sometimes their families, frequently living in loneliness, hounded by the law, and regarding themselves as outcasts.

This sense of shame reaches down into much that so-called normal people do, and creates confusion and inhibitions. American men, in fact, are greatly inhibited by the prevailing sissy complex. Many allow themselves to be deprived of the freedom to partake fully of life and be more complete human beings. They are often ashamed to cry and show love or tenderness, and thus miss meaningful personal communication. Fears that manhood might be questioned often tend to restrict a man's interests, whether it be playing the violin, raising petunias, or dabbling in oils. A man sometimes watches football games on TV or plays poker because these are "safe" activities that fit the accepted definition of masculinity.

For generations, there was a clear-cut social distinction as to which activities were suitable and acceptable for men and which were appropriate for women. But even this did not prevent the development of male homosexuals and lesbians in society, for both are as old as history itself. Sappho, Madame de Staël, and other famous women were known lesbians. Some of the most notable Greek philosophers were deviates. Alexander the Great and Julius Caesar, great generals though they were, had homosexual tendencies and yet rose to power. In a later time, on the other hand, Oscar Wilde was imprisoned for his delinquencies.

Throughout history, men, in order to be thought of as men, have had to play the dominant role. The delicate and creative activities were thought of as feminine and were largely denied to men. A strong patriarchal society existed at the turn of the twentieth century, with the concept of the man being all-powerful. Then social changes came. Women won the right to vote. They bobbed their hair. They shortened their skirts and began to wear trousers (slacks) a good deal of the time. They got jobs in a man's world, learned male occupations, and so on. It has taken men much longer to become involved in what traditionally is women's work, and even today, despite the fact that views are gradually changing, men shy away from becoming ballet dancers for fear they will be regarded as "queer."

It is traditional for a man to preside over the charcoal broiler in the back yard, whereas he is seldom encouraged to develop culinary talents in the kitchen, which is his wife's province. Meat traditionally is a man's concern—a holdover from the days when the head of the household was responsible for killing or trapping the main course for dinner—while other foods are handled by the woman. Many men seem to feel they are asserting their masculinity, while at the same time developing culinary skills, by building a charcoal fire and cooking a steak. This satisfies their wish to cook without its seeming a sissy thing to do.

It is safe to say that a man who is secure in himself as an individual is secure about himself sexually, and therefore is free to develop into a whole person who can cry, cook cheese fondue, enjoy concerts, wash dishes, applaud ballet dancers, attend art exhibits, play the flute or violin, and show compassion for colleagues falling by the wayside in business, as well as watch a football game. Too many men have become ensnared in a masculinity trap that makes them unable to function fully as human beings.

Furthermore, the identity problem is compounded in our society because the images of masculinity and femininity are becoming so confused. The search for personal identity in the sexual context has become increasingly difficult for many of us. There is a great deal of concern that men are not as masculine as they used to be and that women are becoming too aggressive. Many men have become frightened at the prospect of losing their sexual identity to women, but this fear seems to be mainly within themselves, born of increasing freedom for both sexes. This freedom is a result of the fact that the rules as to who should do what are changing, which means people can no longer find role security in certain set activities, as in the past. In developing a new sense of identity, women are following the childhood pattern of behavior, except that instead of imitating their parents, they often are copying what men do. This can make both the imitators and the imitated anxious. The woman who successfully goes through this process, however, eventually has the chance to develop her own identity and remain feminine in the process.

One's attitudes toward sex in general affect his approach to homosexuality. Wainwright Churchill, writing in *Homosexual Behavior Among Males* (Hawthorn Books, 1967, page 156), says, "The American attitude toward male homosexuality has reached such heights of phobia that any behavior that might even tend to suggest homosexual interests is frowned upon and avoided." Because of this phobia born out of fear, ignorance, and insecurity, an act such as an embrace between men, which is acceptable in other societies, is considered inappropriate among American men and sometimes even a sign of overt feelings.

Often without realizing it, we tend to link the fact that homosexual behavior is an immature sexual expression with our own puritanical fears about sex. This produces the half-truths that cause us to make condemnatory generalizations.

Contrary to what many homosexuals say, becoming a homosexual is rarely a matter of free, conscious choice. Sexual development is mistakenly thought of by many as being an either/or condition. There was a time when people thought that you were born with certain sexual predispositions and that they remained with you throughout your life. With the body of knowledge we now have in developmental psychology and psychoanalytic thought, we know that this is not true. Sexual development is a continuum through which we all pass in the course of our early years. It begins with the self-love of infancy and passes through the stage of wanting the parent of the opposite sex for oneself, into the quasi-homosexuality of pre-puberty years when boys and girls appear to spurn one another. The normal progression eventually takes an individual through a period of sexual awakening and into the heterosexual world of adulthood. But in the case of the homosexual, his development is either arrested at a particular point prior to puberty or he reverts to the homosexual stage.

What causes a person to be stalled at one level or to revert to it under certain kinds of stress? Many things may, but it appears that the roles of the parents can be crucial. When combined with the personal nature of the child, a mother's obsession that she should have had a daughter rather than a son can stunt the sexual development of the child, particularly if she makes her feelings known and treats the boy as though he were a girl. Then, too, a parent who abdicates his or her emotional responsibilities in the home is inadequate, and can be a contributing factor. Most of the other things that can happen later, such as seduction by a member of one's own sex, tend to reinforce the sexual problem that has already begun.

In a sense, then, homosexuals suffer from "retarded" or "arrested" emotional development. Parental neglect, rejection, overprotection, overindulgence can all be disturbing influences in disruptions of the continuum of human growth. Sometimes there has been an unusual family situation in which a child has had too much dislike or too much love for one parent. Boys often rebel against masculine domination, girls against their mothers. Sometimes there is no one of the same sex with whom a child can identify. Being seduced by a homosexual in one's youth also can be a traumatic, reinforcing factor. Interestingly, there seems to be a minimum of deviation among men and women who were allowed a degree of sexual freedom while they were growing up.

However, even those who pass through all the stages of development and operate heterosexually may have certain residues of homosexual behavior. Most of us probably have some residual feelings that, strictly speaking, are homosexual in nature. And genetically, we all have male and female hormones, and we have genes transmitted from both parents.

These are not the kinds of things we generally think of in discussing homosexuality, but they are related to the identity crisis. They need not be a cause for fear or problems, for some of these residues can be acceptable socially. For example, as has been noted, it is customary for some European men to kiss each other, whereas Americans shun this sort of thing. In our country, this could be considered a homosexual activity, but it is quite acceptable socially in Europe. There is no reason why men cannot like flowers or show affection as women do.

My own father felt that it was unmasculine for him to carry flowers home to my mother. Once when she was ill, he brought her a bouquet, which he carried behind his back, as though no one would see it there.

All sorts of notions about what is "masculine" and what is "feminine" crop up in our daily lives. When I visited my wife in the hospital after the birth of our first child, I encountered several relatives discussing their views on child-rearing, including a conviction that a father should never change a baby's diaper because this was not "man's work." Some people feel the same way about the man of the house helping with the dishes or other household chores. At the same time, it can be startling to find a housewife repairing the plumbing or tinkering with the engine of the family car.

When it comes to demonstrations of affection between women, we tend to take a more tolerant view. One reason homosexuality in women remains much more hidden than in men is that it is easier to deal with culturally. Scarcely anybody thinks anything of it when two women kiss or dance together or live together.

Overreaction to homosexuality is similar to any other reaction formation. The person who overreacts may be frightened by his own feelings. For example, I know a minister who says, "I can forgive anybody anything, but not a person who is homosexual. That is one sin I can't forgive." If you were to hint that he might be harboring homosexual feelings within himself, it would scare him to death.

In most people's minds, the stereotype of the homosexual appears to be the mincing, effeminate, slim-hipped young man or the mannishly attired woman with closely cropped hair, whereas in reality most people who prefer the social and sexual company of members of their own sex are not significantly different in demeanor or appearance from the average person. Homosexuals are to be found in every racial and religious group, every national group, every economic class and type of neighborhood, and in the city, town, and farmland. There are homosexual truck drivers, clergymen, doctors, corporation presidents, and lawyers, as well as artists, writers, musicians, hairdressers, interior decorators, clothes designers, and actors. Thousands of homosexuals have served with distinction in the armed forces, on school faculties, and in the ministry.

The nation was shocked by the crisis that gripped Walter Jenkins—and as a result, his wife and children, and the official White House family—when it became known that he had been arrested in a YMCA lavatory in Washington on a charge of disorderly conduct involving "indecent gestures." It was not the first time he had faced such an accusation, but never before had such an allegation involving him been publicized.

Walter Jenkins, a trusted member of the White House staff, resigned and returned to his home state of Texas, where he has lived quietly since. His arrest, like the charges leveled by the late Senator Joseph McCarthy linking Communism and homosexuality, stirred considerable discussion about sexual deviation and helped to reinforce efforts to end discrimination against homosexuals in government, the Army, business, and the church.

It is interesting to note that while Jenkins found refuge in a hospital after the scandal was publicized, his neighbors showered his wife and children with love and attention.

Women of the neighborhood helped with the household chores, shopping and cooking for the six Jenkins children.

"It was just the thought," said a neighbor. "They are good people, and we wanted to show them that we were with them. He was a dedicated and hard-working man. . . . We have all had a deep sense of the personal tragedy involved."

President Johnson said: "I have never known a better man, a more diligent worker, a more competent and faithful person. When I heard the story . . . that raised a question about his morals, I was as shocked as if someone had told me that my wife had murdered her daughter. . . . I did the only thing I knew to do—that was to ask for his resignation.

". . . It seems to be a very unfortunate and unpleasant and distressing situation that resulted from intense overwork, and he has my sympathy and my understanding, and his wife and their lovely family have my prayers and my best wishes."

This was not the first time this sort of scandal had shaken high places in Washington, but it was perhaps the first time that the response was one of sympathy as well as condemnation. The neighbors who came to the aid of the Jenkins family, and the President of the United States himself, were in no state of confusion as to where they stood. They were secure enough to speak out in behalf of a friend and colleague who was in trouble.

There have been several cases recently in which government personnel have suffered a great deal personally and professionally because of the general attitude toward homosexuality. (There are hazards in "normality," too. An FBI employee was discharged because a girl had visited his room overnight.) This really indicates not only a problem of the individual but of the government, which is frightened. We still use sexual identity as a form of blackmail. In many instances, work for the government has nothing to do with whether a person is male, female, or homosexual. But apparently the government feels insecure enough to let deviates go. Actually, the philanderer who goes from bed to bed or the woman who flits from man to man is no more reliable. The homosexual appears to be no more or no less reliable than anyone else.

After the Jenkins affair, the American Mental Health Foundation wrote to President Johnson opposing "the kind of hysteria that demands that all homosexual persons be barred from any responsible position." In an issue of *Social Action* magazine, published by the Council for Christian Social Action of the United Church of Christ and devoted entirely to "Civil Liberties and Homosexuality" (December, 1967), one of the writers said, "The government was deprived of an employee who, by all accounts, was a highly qualified Presidential adviser. He and his family were subjected to deep embarrassment, and his friends became suspect. Apart from that, nothing was gained other than a few sensational headlines for the prurient to snicker over." (Permission to use quotation was given by *Social Action*.)

The publication also criticized the church for refusing to help the homosexual, saying: "The church has been the institution most vehement in its opposition to the homosexual. As a result, many if not most homosexuals have, with good reason, felt the church is the last place to turn for understanding and acceptance. . . . The church has failed at the most basic level in its dealings with the homosexual by failing to recognize him as a human being who is sacred in the sight of God. Until those within the church can learn to overcome their aversion to the homosexual, there can be no dialogue, and the homosexual will feel shut out of the house of God."

Most of us choose sides rather than try to ask ourselves what it is that the homosexual is trying to communicate about himself through his sexual attitudes and behavior.

As we have stated, there are various levels of homosexuality and each person has his own individual characteristics and personality to mix with his homosexual tendencies. But there are certain general observations we can legitimately make about the view the homosexual has of himself.

The homosexual's world must remain incomplete, despite what individual homosexuals and their organizations might say. Many homosexuals are unhappy. This, of course, is no criterion in itself because many who are not homosexual are unhappy, too. More to the point, perhaps, is the reason for their unhappiness. Writing of the lot of the homosexual, Edrita Fried, in *The Ego in Love and Sexuality* (Grune & Dutton, 1960, page 103), says: "They [homosexuals] are lonesome strangers who cannot partake of the adult world because, paralyzed in narcissistic solitude, they have remained bereft of the proper means of communicating and relating."

Odd as it may seem, some homosexuals devote their lives to trying to rescue others from this emotionally retarded condition. Such a person came to see me several years ago. As he approached middle age, Jerald acknowledged that he had been actively homosexual since adolescence. Although he had engaged in a few relationships with women, he had never been able to form any lasting attachment for one. Whenever one of these affairs ended, always abruptly, he found a good reason. Either she was too close to her family, had the "wrong" religious, political, or ethnic background, or had some other "shortcoming" that he felt made them incompatible.

Jerald's childhood was spent in a home that provided little love or understanding. His father died when he was seven, and before that time both parents seemed to be constantly in search of themselves. They were tense and anxious to such an extent that Jerald and his two younger siblings were never able to get the kind of parental support or freedom they needed for healthy development. It was difficult for Jerald to express in words the resentment he so obviously felt toward his parents, and for a year and a half of visits to my office he insisted that his parents were the greatest in the world.

As he approached middle age, Jerald began searching, searching for young men he could "rescue" from their plight. They generally came from homes as emotionally insecure as his had been, or more so. Sometimes he would engage in active homosexual relations with these young men, but not always. Since they often engaged in other antisocial behavior, such as stealing, Jerald was in constant jeopardy. He endured robbery, threats, and even blackmail at the hands of the young men he befriended and the hoodlums they brought into his home.

This was self-destruction. As he and I explored the reasons for his behavior pattern, it became increasingly apparent that Jerald was trying to save the young men he saw as carbon copies of himself. In doing so, he hoped to alleviate his own feelings of emptiness and inadequacy. But in each case the relief was only temporary; he had to repeat the experience over and over.

The same kind of situation seems to exist in many female homosexual relationships. Edrita Fried, on page 137 of her book, says that "the oral sex play of lesbian women approximates masturbation more frequently than it represents homosexuality." In these terms, the homosexual may often be described as suffering from an unrequited self-love. His effort to fulfill this infantile emotion is a constant and endless task.

Jerald and many other homosexuals often share with the rigid person the desire to control those around them. Out of the same fear of losing control over the world, some homosexuals constantly try to run things. I knew such a man who wanted those who worked for him to be completely dependent on him. If they dared leave his employ he became violently angry. In his wish to control everything, he became involved in areas in which he lacked ability and competence. As both a homosexual and a rigid person, he failed to establish any durable relationships—in business, in his social life, or sexually.

While it is true that attitudes toward homosexuals are more enlightened today than, say, fifty or a hundred years ago, people still seem to be confused by the existence of deviations and often do not know how to deal with the problem. This is usually a reflection of their own confusion of identity.

Fortunately, psychological and psychiatric help is being made available to growing numbers of homosexuals, and they are showing a willingness to undergo treatment. Also, the church is beginning to come alive to the problem in a constructive way by offering help to homosexuals or homosexually inclined members of the clergy or those seeking seminary training. Many do find assistance through various forms of psychotherapy.

One of the acknowledged deviates I was able to help in therapy was Angus, a brilliant and successful member of the financial community, who felt lonely, unfulfilled, and incomplete. To maintain any concept of his own being, he had to control or be controlled, and thus he was in a state of constant tension. Under a sophisticated and apparently controlled exterior, he saw a hostile world dominated mainly by female images. His feelings were understandable if one was aware of his overcontrolling and emotionally demanding mother and of his father, who had ducked his emotional responsibilities at home by being married to his work. Angus felt a deep hostility to his parents and often projected it on the rest of the world.

In our sessions, we dealt very little with his homosexuality as such, since we regarded it as a symptom rather than a disease—as a way of maintaining a concept of himself. We talked instead about his image of himself as a poor, helpless child in a hostile world. Soon he was projecting his anger at his parents onto me; he wanted to blame me for his situation. When I refused to accept responsibility for his life, while, at the same time, accepting his feelings of anger and frustration, the pattern he had followed for years began to crumble. He slowly came to realize that if I was going to respect him and hold him responsible as an adult, he would have to rethink his feelings about himself.

As his concept of himself improved, he began to engage

less in homosexuality. He began taking women out on dates, and about three years after he first came to see me, he was married and remains so today, apparently quite successfully.

In Angus's case, he used homosexuality to express his state of being in a way that was "safe" for him. He expressed his fears that he could not compete in the heterosexual world, which he often saw as a hostile place.

Lesbians do not seem to seek psychological help as often as male homosexuals do. It seems to be easier for them to function in society, and they are not so willing to acknowledge that there is anything "wrong" with their lives. Also, it may be that they tend to establish more durable relationships than male deviates and therefore have more stable lives.

There can be and often is unhappiness in lesbianism just as in male homosexuality. I know of one case, that of a girl born to middle-aged parents who had counted on having a boy. She was given a boy's name because that is what had been selected in advance, so sure were they that they would have a son. In addition to having a boy's name she was exceedingly unattractive, and she defended herself against unpopularity with boys almost from the outset by seeking the company of girls. She was almost "taught" to be a boy because of her parents' predisposition to have a son. One can look at her homosexuality in terms of its having been a way to please her parents, to do what they wanted. They had wanted a boy, so she would *be* a boy. In the end, of course, they were disappointed, but, oddly enough, they had no idea how it all came about.

One of my failures as a therapist was with an attractive lesbian. Her mother had been dominant, her father a drunk who was away from home most of the time. Her mother continually told her that men were no good, and she could see for herself that her father was not taking any responsibility. The girl dated men and had sexual relations a few times, but she found them unpleasant. To her the aggressive person was her mother. This caused her to think a feminine woman was passive and exploited and could not live with self-respect.

Now, the fact that this girl's effort to find herself failed, while other people have emerged from homosexuality to lead more normal lives, or the simple fact that a person is a homosexual, does not make her (or him) worth more or less as a human being. This identity crisis in the sexual area is just another segment of a wider problem in life.

For the homosexual, as for others with identity problems, the first thing society can do to help is to understand without condemning. Everyone takes sides in his reactions to moral questions. Homosexuals say they have found as good a way of relating as the heterosexual. Actually it does not work that way, for there is a kind of incompleteness in homosexuality.

Today's homosexuals are finding some kind of identity by banding together into organizations to assert their rights. They want to marry, adopt children, enter the armed forces, work in government, and generally achieve equal status with others. While some of their goals are unrealistic, the homosexuals who belong to the Mattachine Society and similar groups are achieving a sense of belonging and of intrinsic worth; these organizations are helping them to lose feelings of guilt and inferiority and are enabling them to function more effectively. Joining an organization will not solve their problems or even help them come to grips with their identity quandaries, how-ever. And it is regrettable that some groups tend to go over-board in trying to convince the rest of the world that there is nothing abnormal about overt deviant behavior, arguing that homosexuals are really acting of their own free will and are in fact members of "the third sex."

This is not an effort to deal with homosexuality in depth; rather, it is an attempt to emphasize its role in the identity crisis. As such, perhaps it will be helpful if we consider our own reactions to homosexuals we meet. People respond in widely different ways, from revulsion to acceptance, with var-ious shades of reactions between—indifference, distaste, and refusal to recognize the existence of homosexuality. How we react tells us a great deal about how we view ourselves. The more secure we feel in our own state of being, the better able we are to accept the homosexual for what he is. One way to consider personal reactions to homosexuality is to look at the extreme measures society proposes. On the one hand, homo-sexuality is a crime, punishable with imprisonment. On the other are groups trying to have the homosexual accepted as a member of the "third sex" without fear or disfavor. Neither extreme can provide much help. The first does nothing to as-sist in personal development; it merely implies that homosex-ual activity is harmful to society. The second bases its argu-ment on a false premise—that there can be a third sex. Since sex is a biological distinction first and a distinction involving attitude second, the position seems to be untenable.

Being judgmental of the activities of others also is a less than ideal posture to assume. When we feel the urge to be judgmental, it may well be because we are a little shaky on our own ground as to our own sex. As with alcohol, if we are too rigid in opposition, it can mean we are too scared to take a drink. In the case of homosexuality, if we protest too much, perhaps we had better pause and take stock of ourselves.

Between Youth and Age

What's wrong with Mom and Dad?

She is either flying off the handle at the slightest provocation or plunged into the dumps. She says no one wants her or needs her anymore and she might as well be dead.

He seems to have suddenly sagged, as though all of the air had been let out of him. He's obviously discouraged, although he doesn't say much, and he is beginning to look old. His one nightly martini before dinner is becoming two, and he's off his golf.

What's the matter?

It is the onset of middle age. Mom is going through the menopause, marking the end of her thirty or more years of fertility. The "change" has set in, dramatically or quietly, but it is taking place. Unfortunately for her, this is happening at the same time the children are leaving home, for school, marriage, and careers, so she really feels bereft.

With men, the changes are in a sense more subtle and less readily acknowledged and accepted than are the biological transformations that spell aging to a woman, but they are there nevertheless. Dad is suffering from fears of financial insecurity in his old age, and he's also concerned—and frightened—over the prospect that his sexual powers are declining. He just doesn't feel that he is as much of a man as he once was and it bothers him a lot.

We put much stress on menopause in jokes, advertisements, and general discussion. Women going through this period in life are often somewhat less than reticent to talk about it than men are. But what happens to men is as important and decisive.

Although I have met few people who are willing to admit they are middle-aged, there is a point in life when none of us can think of himself any longer as young. We may say, "Life begins at forty," or "I don't feel a day over twenty," but in truth we *are* getting older, and these middle years—whether they begin at thirty, forty or fifty—pose some basic problems of identity.

This is the time in life when many men, still spellbound by the American standard of success, wake up one morning and tell themselves they are failures. Failures in whose eyes? I would suppose in most instances it is their own. They did not become President of the United States, a Nobel-prize winning scientist, chairman of the board of General Motors, dean of a college, a Supreme Court Justice, or president-elect of the American Medical Association, even though they were named "the boy most likely to succeed" in their high school senior class. Perhaps they did not rise very high on the mass-produced ladder of success at all, and so, now here they are, forty-five years old, paunchy, baldish, graying, wearing bifocals, having trouble with their teeth, not as raring to go when they awaken in the morning as they were when they were sixteen, and so they feel they are failures.

I recall the first self-styled failure I ever saw. He was a guest at our eating club when I was in college. Old grads frequently joined us at meals and invariably accepted enthusiastically when invited to say a few words. Usually these little talks consisted of glowing reports of their accomplishments, with a big "thank you" for the fine education and great inspiration received at old Alma Mater. One evening we were in for a surprise, however, when our dinner guest got up to speak. He looked older than most of our previous alumni dinner companions, although he was only forty-five. He seemed to exude an aura of defeat as he slowly got up, fumbled with the silverware in front of him, cleared his throat, and said:

"Gentlemen, I am a failure."

He went on to paint a picture of the more than twenty years since his graduation. There had been very few successes —at least according to him—and they were quite minor. But there were many failures, and big ones. So many, in fact, that he finally left the profession for which he had been trained and now he was barely scraping along in a rather dull-sounding job. In our success-oriented culture, Mr. Failure indeed sounded quite accurate in his description of himself. Was he really? If so, did he make himself a failure because he could not measure up to society's criteria of success? The important aspect of what he said was that here he was on the threshold of old age, almost totally devoid of any identity, of any sense of person except that he was a failure.

This experience shocked me. It was the first time I had any real idea that a person might not always accomplish what he set out to do—and be aware that he has missed the boat. I realized, too, also for the first time I suppose, that the great American dream that anybody can become President is a myth, or at least a gross exaggeration. Some of us just don't have what it takes, and instead of being able to accept it and settle for what we *can* do, we succumb to the word *failure*. Moreover, I realized that the absence of success with a capital "S" might be enough for a person to consider himself a failure when, even in terms of our culture, he may be neither or he may be, on the qualitative scale, more of a success than a failure. Actually the concept of success is not so much the degree to which we meet certain social criteria of success as it is the degree to which we fulfill our own wishes, desires, abilities, and dreams. Therefore it is not correct to think of ourselves—or anyone else—as *either* a success or a failure. In most cases, we are a combination of both; we achieve some of the things we hoped to and we have not been able to attain others.

While most men do not experience such a complete lack of accomplishment and such a deep loss of self-confidence as this man, there is a time in the middle years when we have to accept our own finiteness and mortality and recognize that there may be some limitations to what we can do. For many men, this period poses a kind of identity crisis that wreaks havoc with their middle years and makes them miserable in their old age—if they live that long.

I once knew a man who, rather than telling himself he was a failure, heard the verdict from his son, a bright young man with the kind of false standards that are instilled in children as they are egged on to excellence in everything, particularly in the capacity to earn money. This boy, while still in college, looked at his father one day and asked him: "Dad, why are you a failure?" The question haunted the father for the rest of his life; now his son is middle-aged and no more successful than his father. He, in turn, is haunted by the memory of that searing question, when in actuality both *were* at least moderately successful by anyone's standards.

A sense of failure is what brought Fred, a forty-two-year-old draftsman, to see me, at the suggestion of his boss. Fred was adequate at his job until he received a promotion making him a supervisor with several men under him. His own supervisor had shown some reluctance to give him the new responsibility, but Fred had seniority and he appeared to be ambitious, asking frequently for a chance to prove what he could do. So his boss gave him the opportunity when it arose.

Fred became acting supervisor for what was to have been a trial period, after which he was to receive a permanent promotion. As soon as he assumed the post, he began to feel anxious. He couldn't sleep. His appetite diminished. He was nervous and cross. He made mistakes he had never made before, and his work was not as productive as it should have been. At first, his supervisor was going to remove him from his new assignment, but when this possibility was mentioned, Fred became agitated and visibly upset.

"This is my one chance at being *somebody*," he said. "If you take it away from me, I'll be a failure."

Sensing there was more at stake than success or failure in a particular job, Fred's supervisor wisely asked me if I would talk to him, and I agreed. When he came to my office, Fred was on the edge of despair. As he talked, it became increasingly apparent that his whole concept of himself as a person was bound up in making a success of his new job. It became evident, too, that he had been given little opportunity to experience himself as a person at home, where he was constantly badgered by his wife's demands and complaints, with which he had never learned to deal adequately. Because he regarded himself as a failure as a person at home, he had unconsciously decided that work would have to be the place where his self-concept was made or broken. Unfortunately he lacked the required skills and emotional strength to cope with a position of responsibility. This combination was too much for him.

He and I talked at great length about the idea that his worth as a person was not really bound up in his job. This displeased him. He said repeatedly, "Look at me. I'm forty-two. What have I accomplished?" My constant effort was to try to communicate to him that I was neither impressed nor disinterested in what he had or had not accomplished but that I respected him as a person, as Fred.

Eventually his supervisor had no choice but to remove him from his position of responsibility, and it became evident that Fred would remain at the same job level during the rest of his working life. I could not lead him to believe he was going to become the company president, when obviously he was not, but at the same time, I did try to help him accept himself as a person of worth, regardless of the level at which he was functioning. Fred could not listen and so, in a sense, remained lost.

Many men are confronted in the middle years with the need to bridge the gap between dream and accomplishment. Some, of course, become aging Walter Mittys, gaining self-importance from living in a dream world filled with high adventure. Others cannot accept the fact they did not "make the grade" and so become disgruntled and disheartened. It is hoped that most look back without anger and settle for what they are, thankful they fared as well as they did.

There is a joke about men becoming anxious on their fortieth birthdays. This is not without meaning, for it is at about this point that self-concept must be separated from accomplishment without denigrating accomplishment or implying that most men do not make substantial contributions during and after middle age. Rather, it should be a time to separate oneself from one's dreams and at some point be able to make a realistic appraisal of where one has been and where one is going.

Women also face problems as their children grow up and leave home, often forcing Mom to change her entire way of life and as a result to alter her identity. Harriet G. was one of these women. She was in a state when she came into my office. She said she did not know what her problem was, but that "the bottom seemed to have dropped out of everything" in only a few months. Life seemed to have lost its meaning. She was listless, and it seemed pointless for her to try to go on.

We talked about many things and finally got to the crux of her difficulty when she told me that the previous autumn her fourth and youngest child had gone off to school in a distant city, leaving her "unemployed," so to speak. She described in great detail the attention she had given the children while they were growing up. It became evident that for two decades her every waking hour had been devoted to the care and rearing of four children. As she passed from youth to middle age she remained unaware—or unwilling to accept—the fact that one day the children would be out on their own. Her life had been so wrapped up in them that they, in a sense, had become her identity. When they were gone, it was as though her very being had gone with them, leaving her an empty person.

It is one of the small tragedies of American life that this is not an uncommon story. While many mothers weather rather well the transition from a full house to a relatively empty one, many do not. For some, the reaction is even more devastating than it was for Harriet. There are those who, in their acute loneliness, begin to drink too much, become withdrawn and morose, or turn to sexual promiscuity as an outlet. Some seem to fall apart physically as well as psychologically. The woman with some sense of identity either prepares in advance for the period when she is no longer a professional mother by developing skills, hobbies, or job qualifications, or deals with the problem when it occurs by substituting something for the void. There are of course those who go through a rather trying period of using clothes, frequent visits to the beauty parlor, or endless physical culture "kicks" to make up for the absence of children from the house. These, at best, are temporary substitutes.

Harriet's problem, as is the case with many others, was that she was too involved with her children. This may seem to be a curious viewpoint, especially to dedicated mothers, for when children are very small their needs and wants are great, and most of them must be provided by the mother. Yet Harriet, in a sense, had developed the feeling that she and her children were one. She was not aware of this feeling until they had left, and even then she was not precisely sure where the feeling sprang from or what it meant.

Why does this happen so often and what can be done about it? There are several factors, cultural and personal, that lead many women to react as Harriet did. One is a deeply embedded feeling in the unconscious recesses that one's own dependency needs have never been satisfied. When this happens in this kind of woman, her extreme involvement with her children unconsciously becomes comparable to putting money in the bank. The unconscious then reasons something like this: "If I am good to them and make them my everything, then I will be sure that I will never be alone and never feel alone. They are my insurance for being. As long as they are near, I know that I *am*. They will care for me, support me, and love me, and I will never have to face the anxiety of feeling alone." She is, in a sense, equating herself with her children. The problem is complicated by the fact that these are unconscious feelings. A woman generally does not know she has them. If you suggested to her that she might feel this way, she probably would be genuinely horrified, upset, and perhaps even angry.

Another factor that sometimes contributes to the development of this kind of feeling is a general cultural attitude that a parent (and particularly a mother) should give up everything for a child. This is the sort of thing we used to see advocated in women's magazines, but it is so much cultural garbage to think that a mother "should" give up her entire being and right of privacy for her child. I must add that it is as bad

for the child as for the mother, for this kind of human sacri-
fice can make the child either overdependent or abnormally
resentful of his mother. We are producing these two extremes
of feeling in our child-centered culture in which Mother has
allowed herself to be the lowest-paid, hardest-working servant
in the country.

I cannot help but feel that to a large extent the excessive
"should" demand stems from either a real resentment of one's
children or a feeling of never having actually accomplished
anything as a person, apart from childbearing. While children
need attention and guidance, the mother who is able to give
them without surrendering her identity to the roles of chief
cook and chauffeur need not feel abandoned and alone when
the children are gone, and she will be much more interesting
to visit—and be visited by—if she can present herself as an
individual with some interest in life outside the nursery, play-
room, family room, and kitchen.

In many instances this problem is aggravated by the fact
that over the years the parents have drifted apart. The father
has been so involved in work, in advancing himself in pursuit
of the great American dream, that he has had little time for
his wife. She, on the other hand, compensates for this by sub-
merging herself in her children, perhaps even sacrificing the
marriage by becoming so involved with the children that she
has had little time or desire to share life with him. As com-
pensation for her neglect of him, he may be driven deeper
into his work; it can also drive him to drink, to increasing
travel, or to other women. In any case, when she no longer
has the children to fill her time, she looks as a last resort to
her husband, only to find herself facing a stranger—and he is

confronted by the household drudge and governess. Her feelings of loneliness, emptiness, and uselessness are then compounded, and sense of failure is not alleviated.

As in most of life, the best answer in such a situation is to strive to achieve and maintain a sense of balance. Just because a mother bears and rears children does not mean she owns them forever. The mother who can see that her children are people in their own right, who need love, attention, and affection, but who also have a right to grow up and an obligation to leave to fulfill their own destinies has a much better chance of escaping this kind of quandary. She will be the kind of person who does not lose sight of her obligation to herself—even in the periods when the needs and demands of the children are greatest. She may be limited in the time she has for herself, but she need not be restricted in her insistence on her own right to privacy and state of personal being.

One of the situations—and it is *only* one—that confronts women in the middle years and that often has a great bearing on their concepts of themselves is the menopause blues, which on the surface can be more dramatic and traumatic than the fearful forties are for men. Menopause is inevitable, and just as inevitably it will pass, with or without the blues, while the depression that can afflict the aging man is more subtle and can actually be more prolonged.

A great deal is made of the biological transformation called menopause. It is natural that this change in body chemistry, bringing about a gradual waning of the ability to reproduce, should have a profound effect. Feelings that accompany menopause often are physiological, but they also can be emotional. These emotions may exist in the woman who has not had children as well as in the one who has had several. Menopause can leave the barren woman feeling incomplete and sometimes gives her a sense of having *been* useless—a failure in her "job" as a woman, in the same sense that her husband may feel he has failed because he has not produced success in business.

One of the first things to accept about menopause is that it is not a sickness, although there are people, including a doctor who wrote a best-seller on the subject, who have branded it a "disease." Rather, this period, usually occurring between the ages of forty and fifty, is part of the natural life process. It *has* to happen. And it is bound to be accompanied or followed by physiological changes. As the ovaries go out of business, other glands do go to work in a kind of compensatory action; as the ovarian production of the female hormone estrogen diminishes, a change of chemical balance occurs, often producing what are known as hot flushes, or flashes. At the same time, an increase in the production of male hormones by the adrenal gland can result in the growth of hair on the face, and a decrease in breast size. Often the changes produce an accumulation of fatty deposits in unwelcome places. The duration of menopause may be short or long. It may be experienced with little or no discomfort or discussion, or with great and dramatic distress. Some women actually welcome it as a kind of "liberation." Part of what happens depends on the individual and her ability to withstand change. Part of it is beyond her control in terms of her feelings, emotions, and attitude toward herself and others. When a woman does not identify her state of being with her sex or her ability to bear children, the adjustments to these changes can be accomplished with much more ease.

It is not unusual for women to experience considerable emotional upheaval at this time. Some of the trauma may have a physiological basis, while other aspects of it may be rooted in the psychology of the individual woman. Symptoms of disquietude include depression, anxiety, and a certain degree of apprehension. To a considerable extent, the severity of these emotional reactions to menopause depends on the individual. While some women have developed their whole concept of self in the fact that they were able to bear children, as has been stated, others who because of neurotic conflicts have never been able to marry and bear children may also experience a great deal of emotional discomfort.

Mary K. was one of these women. She never married because "the right man did not come along," and so she had been in a state of emotional conflict all her life. As she approached menopause, two things happened. First, the physiological changes accentuated her long-standing problems. And, second, because she had always claimed she *wanted* to marry and have children, she now felt she had "frittered away" her life. Before she knew it, the time for having children had passed and she was faced with the onset of older age without being able to reproduce. As she expressed her feeling, "It's as though my being a woman was something I had waited for all my life and now it's passed even before it began."

As we talked about Mary's past, a picture emerged of a girl who had never grown up, who remained tied to her parents well beyond the appropriate time ("devotion," she called it), and who, consequently, had lost, on an emotional level at least, what could have been the most fulfilling phase of her life. Naturally we could not reverse the process of aging; we could not help Mary go back and regain the time and experience she had lost. We could help her only through the remainder of her life, perhaps enabling her to learn something from the emotional mistakes she had made before. We could, perhaps, help her learn to realize that she was a person whether or not she had borne children.

Not every emotional upheaval of middle-age is so hard on a woman. There are those who come to feel that this period may produce very positive, salutary results. Gladys was such a woman. Although a good mother and devoted to her family, she had harbored feelings of resentment since childhood. She felt she had been given too much responsibility too young and, in fact, she had. Throughout her life, her feelings of resentment and frustration were vague. During menopause they became more pronounced, which frightened her at first but also gave her a real chance to understand and deal with these feelings. By taking advantage of this opportunity, her future promises her more internal freedom than she has ever had before in her life.

Women who already have emotional problems may find them exaggerated during menopause, but some discover that the change gives them new sexual freedom.

When emotional problems do occur during this period, husband and family can be of considerable assistance if only by understanding what is happening to Mother. Patience, silence, and love are called for. In some instances, it is best to simply ignore the process, and then she will not make it a topic of conversation. Showing love toward the middle-aged woman so decisively losing her youth is the most effective way to help —and love can go a long way toward supporting the perplexed and discouraged middle-aged man, too, as well as the teen-ager going through adolescent trauma, or anyone else with an identity problem.

It is important for friends and relatives of the woman going through menopause to realize that her changes of mood are not directed at them. They may not be aimed at anyone at all. It helps if the bystanders can avoid taking little outbursts too personally, and if they understand that the process of menopause is natural and inevitable and is happening to just about everyone else's middle-aged wife and mother who has not undergone gynecological surgery. A physician can help by prescribing medication that curbs feelings that are physiological in origin, and hot flushes are curable or obviated by easy-to-take hormone pills.

Most important in this period is the attitude of the woman herself. She must remain aware that her concept of herself as a person and as a woman is vital. She has to convince herself that she is a woman not only to bear children. She who feels she gets her identity from her fertility falls into the same emotional trap as the man who identifies himself with his job. Both are persons apart from what they do or produce.

Middle age can be traumatic for all of us. We have looked at only a few samples of the identity crises that people may— and often do—experience in middle age. It is a time of change—but then, so is most of life. Perhaps it is the time when we finally realize that we are finite, that we will not live forever. We may not have become as powerful, famous, or wealthy as we thought we might when we were young. Now we are confronted with the prospect of perhaps compromising a bit with our dreams, our hopes, and even our little self-delusions.

Remember you are not alone in this plight. You have most of your contemporaries in the world for company. A reasonable sense of self therefore is of paramount importance for the middle years, if the time that lies ahead is to be meaningful and productive, and if you are to be *you* for as long as you live.

10

The Crisis of the Aged

Mary MacNeal lay tossing in the dark, as she had for more nights than she could count. At almost the same time every night, she had been awakened by the same disquieting dream. In it, her mother had been abandoned and was crying out in the darkness. The cries always awakened Mary before she could go to her mother's rescue, and the nightmare preyed on her mind during her waking hours.

Mary knew all too well what the problem was. She did not need a psychologist or psychiatrist to tell her why her mother lay heavy on her mind, conscious and subconscious. Mary's mother—and in turn, Mary—was going through a phase of life that confronts millions of us. Her mother was passing from being a normally functioning person into senility.

It was difficult for Mary to accept that her mother was becoming a different person from the self-reliant, active, interesting homebody she had been during most of her adult life.

Whenever anyone was sick, Mary's mother had provided loving care. She had kept her own house, reared four children, been attentive to her husband, belonged to clubs, read avidly, subscribed to concerts, and devoted considerable energy to her garden. After her children were grown, she maintained an active interest in them and her grandchildren, and when her husband retired she traveled with him and otherwise kept busy. Then, at sixty-eight, Carl Williams died, and nothing was ever quite the same again. It was as if his wife had lost her purpose in life, although she did not show any outward signs of morbid mourning.

Now, at seventy-one, Mrs. Williams was becoming forgetful. She tended to tell the same anecdotes frequently, and her personality seemed to be undergoing subtle changes. For one thing, she paid less attention to her appearance and did not putter around the garden much anymore. One day while out shopping she could not remember how to get home, and a store clerk had to call a policeman to take her the few blocks to her front door. There were times, too, when she engaged in pointless arguments over the most trivial things, and she had become almost unbearably inquisitive about the lives of her neighbors and her children.

Mary discussed the situation with her husband, John, and they decided that something might have to be done. Just what, they were not prepared to say, but they felt that her mother could not go on as she was without some kind of attention. Perhaps the family doctor could help, so Mary suggested that her mother make an appointment with him. She accepted this readily and saw the doctor regularly. At each visit he gave her a prescription for some "little pills" and reassured her there was nothing wrong. He told Mary the pills were just to calm the old lady's nerves and also would help to satisfy her need for attention.

Mrs. Williams continued to deteriorate, however. She refused to have anyone come in to clean her house although neglecting it herself. When Mary tried to tidy things a little and dust the furniture, her mother objected.

Clearly *something* had to be done. Mary talked to John about it and telephoned her sister and brothers who lived a long distance away. They all agreed that they would have to take action if their mother continued to go downhill. This is what was on Mary's mind when she went to bed at night and when she awakened at 4 A.M. with her mother's cries ringing in her ears.

What to do?

Friends suggested that a possible solution might be a nursing home or a residence for elderly people. Mary balked at such ideas. She had been reared in a family where "shunting old people aside" was not considered acceptable treatment, and she felt extremely guilty at the mere thought. However, it became increasingly clear that ultimately this was what was going to have to happen. Mary and John could not bring her mother into their home for a number of reasons, and her mother had said repeatedly through the years she would not live with any of her children under any condition.

Mary was plagued not only by the problem of what a good and dutiful daughter should do. Her worries were complicated by the fact that with increasing frequency she became annoyed and even angry with her mother. It was frustrating to be around a person who often could not remember from one moment to the next what the topic of conversation had been, and it was distressing to visit a home that was becoming messier and messier. Added to this was Mary's embarrassment when police and others occasionally brought her mother home from downtown because she had forgotten where she was. Mrs. Williams's eating habits were deteriorating, too, and Mary was concerned about her physical health and the possibility she might be suffering from malnutrition, which occurs in many old people who live alone.

Like so many of the twenty million old people in our country, Mary's mother was going through a kind of identity crisis. Senility had set in. With senility, a person's entire personality and world view change. Also, one's concept of oneself may change. Some people become childlike, others merely forgetful, but whatever happens, there is no way back from the gradual process of disengagement from life, physically as well as psychologically, with the final disengagement being death. Physically as one grows older he may not hear or see as well as he did, his skin becomes wrinkled, and he shrinks in stature. His reactions become slower and he is less agile. Deep organic and chemical changes take place as well. Many of the changes through which a person passes as he becomes older are physiological. We know, for example, that hardening of the arteries can have a profound effect on a person's emotional outlook.

Moreover, the range of the old person's interests and activities tends to lessen as his circle of friends and relatives diminishes. There are fewer and fewer people with whom he can communicate in terms meaningful to him, and the world becomes in a sense a foreign land that is filled with strangers whom he cannot understand. He begins to feel isolated and perhaps frightened. To compensate for this, the old person often begins to lay great store in the possessions surrounding him, which become like old friends. This explains one reason why so many old people keep belongings that their children regard as useless junk when it is time to break up the family home.

These things were happening to Mary's mother in her final identity crisis. But there was another crisis of identity, too. The onset of senility often produces personality problems for members of the family. Indeed, Mary was plunged into her own identity crisis with the loss of her mother as she had always known her. Suddenly Mary realized she was without a parent, and yet her parent still lived. It had been easier to accept the death of her father than the changes that had come over her mother, changes so great that mother and daughter were reversing positions, with the daughter now being mother and the mother being the child.

Mary keenly missed not being able to share any more little confidences with her mother, for there was no assurance that her mother could keep any kind of secret. It was impossible to seek her mother's advice. She, instead, was guiding her mother, and she had to force herself to realize that the situation could only get worse, never better. She also had to try to maintain her own feeling of identity while helping her mother retain at least a modicum of self-respect.

Finally, after conferences with the doctor, the minister, and the rest of the family, the decision was made to sell Mary's mother's house and arrange for her to move to a nursing home where she would receive the proper constant care and possibly find companionship. The task of breaking up the family home was painful, for it meant disposing of sixty years' accumulation of "treasures" that in themselves had given Mrs. Williams part of her sense of identity. Mary's mother seemed to accept the idea of the change although she complained about it once in a while. She finally settled down in one of the nation's 25,000 homes for the aged where between 500,000 and 750,000 men and women are receiving care. (Another 1,250,000 are invalids who cannot get along without help from others, with a total of more than twelve million old people suffering from at least one chronic condition such as high blood pressure, arthritis, diabetes, heart disease, or mental disorder. This picture is a formidable one, and it becomes more so when you consider that in the next fifteen or twenty years, the total population of aged Americans is expected to reach twenty-five million, which means that unless medical science finds a way to combat the vicissitudes of old age, the number of ailing, hospitalized, and otherwise dependent aged people will be enormous.)

The Marys who have taken the step of helping their parents into nursing homes have had to go through difficult days and nights in reaching this decision. In moving her mother, Mary had to ask herself if this meant that her mother was less of a person than she had been. Certainly not. While it was clear that this was the best thing for her mother, did it infringe on her rights as a person? Not as long as her mother agreed to the change. Had she objected, some other alternative might have been necessary.

When one considers moving a relative to a home for the aged, he should try to see both sides. Many nursing homes and other establishments for old people are fine places, and when a person reaches the point where he cannot care for himself, as Mary's mother did, it is incumbent on the children to see that adequate care is provided.

Children ask themselves, "Should I take my mother into my house?" "Should she go to a nursing home?" "Should I hire a nurse or companion to live with her?" These are tough questions, and quite understandably they made Mary anxious, angry, and even a little guilty. They evoked a combination of feelings that somehow threatened Mary's own identity. First she was confronted with the realization that her mother was a different person than she had been. Then she was faced with what she considered to be the demands of society as she saw it—that a loving and dutiful daughter should manage somehow to take her mother into her own home. The financial burdens of care for the elderly also entered into the situation. So did the possibility that her mother might eventually resent having to live in a nursing home and therefore make a poor adjustment to it.

But the decision was made, and Mary's mother was settled in a nursing home, where she continued to go downhill. Mary's own identity crisis deepened. She became a different kind of person, too. Now that she no longer had her mother with her, she went through the kind of mourning that comes with permanent separation from a loved one. She went through all the anxiety, grief, and guilt that often go with a death, and these were heightened by the fact that Mary visited her mother frequently, took her driving, and brought her home for dinner, all the while seeing her as the ghost of what she had once been.

Occasionally, her mother would say, "I can't understand

why I can't go home again. I took care of my own mother to the day she died. I don't know why I have to be here. I guess the modern generation just doesn't care about old folks."

Now, it is true that for some people it is an easy way out to be able to send a senile parent to a nursing home or some other institution. These are not the people we are discussing here, and we hope they are in a minority. We are talking about the children who are faced with a genuine problem when their parents start going downhill. While it is natural for one to feel guilty, it is not always justified. There may be many practical considerations and other reasons as well why it is desirable to have a senile old person in an institutional environment. This is particularly true if there are children or if both husband and wife work, as was the case with Mary and John. Also, old people may need a kind of care that is not available at home, and many homes for the aged—often called "convalescent hospitals" for some ironic reason—offer recreation and occupational therapy that keep people busier than if they were at home. Then, too, if a person needs constant supervision it is better to provide it in a professional atmosphere. This is not to say that all nursing homes are good. Some of them are quite bad, but there are many that provide a good environment and care for old people, and more are being built every day.

So far, we have been discussing only the extreme cases. The crisis that leads to a nursing home is a severe one in the lives of parents and children. Not everyone who becomes elderly goes to a nursing home or needs to go to one, but we tend to segregate even those old people who are able to remain in society. In our culture, we have resolved the "problem" of old people in our midst with Golden Age clubs, etc. These have their value, of course, but only a limited one, for they set old people aside and prevent younger generations from having the opportunity of sharing the wisdom and experience that only a long life can provide. They also keep older people from sharing in the problems, joys, and experiences of the younger generations.

While we Americans tend to denigrate old age, this is not true of all cultures. The Orientals, for example, respect age and permit their old people to lapse gracefully into a second childhood. The old Japanese are allowed to don the red coats of childhood when they reach the age of eighty and they are revered and accepted as being in their second childhood.

It requires a great deal of patience to be with a senile person. Impatience only serves to make him feel anxious. He does not understand why you are aggravated, and you pay a price for the aggravation within yourself. I know a young woman whose ninety-year-old great-grandmother lived with her family. She was a pleasant person to be with, but became quite forgetful in her advanced years and told the same stories over and over, usually about events far in the past. When my friend was a teen-ager, the old lady would chat with her every morning while she combed her hair and prepared to go to school. And every morning, the great-grandmother would tell exactly the same story about her daughter—my friend's grandmother—losing all her curly hair in a bout with scarlet fever. The hair grew back, but straight. And every morning, my friend would react as though she had never heard the story before. Had she become impatient, it would not have helped, for Grandma would have continued to tell the story anyway.

In instances such as this, it may be best to think and talk as though in the company of a small child. All of us are patient with the little one who has to have something explained several times or who repeats himself constantly. Why can't we show the same consideration for an old person? For example, when Junior plays with his teddy bear as though it is alive, we don't say, "That's ridiculous." We join in treating the bear as a live creature. This same attitude can be taken toward a senile old person without threatening our own self-esteem.

There are, of course, countless illustrations of people who have lived to a great age and continued to be active and alert and contribute to society all the while. Herbert Hoover was one of these men. So was Bernard Baruch. Winston Churchill did not really come into his own until he was in his sixties and World War II put demands on him that drew him to greatness. Dwight D. Eisenhower was seventy when he left the White House.

For a variety of reasons we have tended to make sixty-five the arbitrary cutoff point for putting people on the shelf. There is always the possibility that challenges will keep people going, however. In a report on "The Older Generation," the President's Council on Aging had this to say:

"For many retired people, nothing is quite so difficult—or quite so important—as maintaining a useful and congenial place in the community around them. . . . The Older American retires from his job to face reduced income, loss of regular contact with his work companions, rupture of a pattern of life built up over decades—and free time. Perhaps for the first time since childhood, there are extra hours—hours with no demands, perhaps hours in which he can find nothing to do.

"This is retirement. This is a sudden new way of life for the Older American. He has a different role in society and in his family relations. His self-image is bound to change in some fashion. At the worst, it erodes into a state that has been called 'retirement shock.' "

While for some people retirement may prove to be the most fruitful period of their lives and poses no identity crisis, too many find themselves castoffs in a society where production and achievement are among the top virtues. There are almost classic cases of people who have died shortly after retirement. Not long ago, for example, Wayne Johnston, president of the Illinois Central Railroad, died in his easy chair six days after he retired. A newspaper executive retired, said his farewells, and went home and dropped dead not an hour later. I know of another case in which a prominent lawyer died six months after his retirement and to this day no one is certain what killed him.

An alert, interesting old lady I knew moved into a nursing home at the age of eighty because she had no family and was lonely. She ran errands for those who were bedridden or unable for other reasons to go out. One day, this active, alert woman fell on her way to a nearby drugstore. She was able to make her way back to the nursing home and an examination disclosed no injuries, but she went to bed that day and never got up again. She would lie for hours with her face to the wall and simply gave up, apparently having decided never to get up again so that she would never fall again.

Something comparable happens to some mothers when their children grow up and leave home, as we have seen in the preceding chapter. With their jobs at an end, their incentive is gone and this plunges them into an identity crisis. Something keeps you young as long as children are around. First, you need physical energy to cope with lively youngsters. Like an athlete who keeps in trim, the parent, and sometimes the grandparent, needs to be in shape. When the football player stops playing, he tends to get flabby if he is not careful. Parents and grandparents no longer actively involved in rearing children get psychologically as well as physically flabby.

We are going to have a heightening of the identity crisis of old age as time goes on. As the retirement age gets lower, to make room for the young people who are coming along, more people are going to be put on the shelf unless they find something challenging, interesting, or useful to do, or unless they are helped in this search.

Many people are managing to keep occupied, gainfully and otherwise, in their later years. A Navy officer I know was separated from the service at the age of sixty. As far as he was concerned, he was retired, and he rather liked the idea. He felt, however, that he needed something to do to keep occupied, so he applied for a job as a factory gatekeeper. When the personnel director read his application form, he called the man in and said: "You are overqualified to be a gatekeeper and you are too young to retire. We need you in management." So the retired Navy officer became an executive of the company and is still going strong and enjoying every minute of it.

There was no such happy resolution to Carl O.'s retirement problem, however. At his retirement after forty years, he had worked his way up from an hourly paid packer to head of a department in a manufacturing concern. His departure was marked with a departmental dinner and the usual parting gifts and words of praise from management. Carl made a little speech in which he said he was looking forward to escaping from the "rat race" of business and would be glad to sit at home and rest for a while.

Only a few weeks passed before Carl started dropping in at the plant, "just to say hello" or because "I was in the neighborhood." His former co-workers noticed that he did not look as robust as he had. They asked about his health but he assured them that his doctor only recently had found him in excellent condition. When asked what he was doing with his time, he replied, "Nothing." Nine months later, Carl died of a heart attack.

"In a sense it didn't surprise me," said one of his former assistants. "Every time I saw him he kept saying there was nothing for an old man to do and that once a man retires, he might as well be dead."

George B.'s story had a happy ending. He, too, had to retire at the mandatory age of sixty-five. He had worked hard and was devoted to his job, but he was able to deal with his identity in retirement without a crisis. After taking life easy for a few months, he became restless. His health was good and he wanted something to do. He knew that he had to become active in something that would sustain his interest over a long period of time.

His daughter and son-in-law knew of his wishes in this matter, so it was no frivolous matter when they sent him several orchid plants from Hawaii. They knew he had always admired orchids and decided he might take up raising them as a hobby. George took the bait. He built a greenhouse and became active in local florist organizations. His plants frequently won prizes—and he also found an entire new circle of friends. One day as we were boarding a plane, George gave my wife one of the most beautiful white orchids I have ever seen. It was one of his prizes.

While continuing his interest in orchids, George's activities branched out. He and his wife made a trip to Arizona where they picked up some semiprecious stones. When he returned home, he began learning how to polish them, which led to a second hobby—the finding, cutting, and polishing of semiprecious stones. He built a workshop in a shed behind his house where he makes gifts for his friends and relatives. George and his wife became members of the local Rockhounds Group, and though he is in his eighties and she in her seventies, they have bought a trailer for their rock-hunting trips. Here is a fine example of a man who retired from a job, but not from life.

Encouraging older people to remain as active as possible so they can stay interested in being alive is the chief thing we can do for them, beyond helping them economically and in other ways. It is important that we enable them to keep a concept of their own worth. Much can be accomplished through the Golden Age clubs, and there also are communities for senior citizens, such as Leisure World, in Southern California, which are designed to provide a well-rounded life of social and occupational involvement, albeit segregated in a sense from the rest of society.

The National Association of Retired People has been organized by and for older people. It was started by members of the National Association for Retired Teachers and provides a variety of information and services including the sale of reduced-rate drugs and medicines, organization of tours and cruises geared to the slower pace of older people, and provision of advice on insurance and leisure time pursuits. Through its magazine, *Modern Maturity,* the organization tries to encourage and enhance respect for the pursuits and accomplishments of the elderly and to make the older people feel a sense of worth.

There are times when special services are needed for the elderly friends or relatives who cannot cope with some of the simple, everyday demands of living but at the same time are able to remain in their own homes or apartments. Although these services are still limited, communities in forty states provide homemaker services through funds allocated by the Federal Government. Homemakers visit the homes of elderly people a few hours each week to help with cleaning and cooking and to do the shopping. A few communities have services that provide prepared meals for the aged at nominal costs. These are known as Meals on Wheels.

Recently, a foster-family care plan for the aged was launched. Its purpose is to provide an adequate environment for older people to spare them from the isolation of living alone or from the deteriorating effects that institutions can have. Communities with such programs have established standards much as they have for foster care of children, with the foster families being carefully screened and every effort made to ensure a pleasant and emotionally stable atmosphere.

There are other aids for older people. They include counseling and social casework; family counseling; protective social, medical, and legal services; information and referral services; shopping services; visiting services; night sitting, transportation, and personal care.

All of these services take into account the fact that the older person is not the person he once was; in fact, that is the very basis for their existence. It often is difficult for the increasingly helpless recipient of aids to the elderly to accept assistance gracefully, whether from friend, relative, or stranger. The changes that have taken place within himself and in his life are difficult to take. The fact that they herald the end of the human course sometimes makes them doubly hard to take.

For ourselves, as we watch someone we love going downhill, the more secure we are in our own identity, the more gracefully we can accept this decline. At the same time, we need to remember that the object of our concern remains a person—a changed and changing person, even as we, too, are changing constantly with the passage of time.

11

"She Was My Life"

The facts of death—the high cost of funerals and the widespread exploitation of the bereaved—have become as widely known as the facts of life. The funeral director has been exposed in books and articles, on television and in newspapers, as a kind of Simon Legree, out to bleed the families of the deceased of every cent he can get. The commercialization of death has been extended to a sickening output of greeting cards expressing the "he is not dead" philosophy. Clergymen also have contributed to the deplorable exploitation of the bereaved through often-misguided efforts to soften the blow of death by denying it exists or glossing it over.

The mortician, the cemetery owner, the greeting card manufacturer, and the minister are all guilty, in their way, of taking advantage of those who find they must plan and pay for funerals. Criticism is warranted, to be sure, but are the abuses of the funeral rite *all* their fault? Can't some of the blame be placed on the shoulders of the bereaved themselves? You need only look around to see plenty of people who *want* ornate funerals with expensive caskets, mountains of floral tributes, and elaborate ceremonies for their loved ones. Are we not justified, therefore, in asking whether the public has not to some extent *allowed* itself to be victimized by the funeral industry?

This leads to another question: Why?

Why do people go to extremes in planning funerals? Why are they willing to be exploited, to go into debt, and to lay themselves bare to the glare of public grief? Obviously the entire concept of death, how we deal with it, and how we react to it fits into the way we meet life and think of ourselves. What Jessica Mitford has called "the American way of death" is one of the major symptoms of our national identity crisis.

In their efforts to *"be* somebody," many people feel that they must arrange elaborate funerals for their loved ones. Whether they admit it or not, they are afraid of public opinion; they think that if they fail to provide "the best," they are making a public admission that they do not care. In addition, they may be concerned lest others think they could not afford an elaborate funeral, therefore attaching to themselves the stigma of financial failure. How often have you heard a person say, "What will 'they' think if we don't do our best for Dad?" What is he really saying? He may be indicating that his concept of himself is bound up in how much he can "show off" to others, even at a time of grief. He may also be disclosing that rather than caring so much for Dad, he actually held him in little regard; by making a big show he is spared from acknowledging that he really may not have cared very much.

Sociologically, the funeral is a rite of passing; it marks the passage from life. All cultures have had rites for the passing from childhood to puberty, from puberty to marriage, and so on. Therefore one of the constructive purposes of the funeral can be to help people accept and acknowledge that a person is dead. It is the last act in the drama of living—a kind of punctuation mark.

It seems that the most appropriate way to deal with this period and with making final arrangements is to do so in a manner consistent with the rest of one's life, one's relationship with the person who has died and the circumstances of the deceased's life. If the man who has died was of modest means, it would be inappropriate to bury him in an expensive bronze casket. If, indeed, you insisted on doing so it would be appropriate to ask what it was you were trying to convey by such inappropriate behavior. You might be indicating an identity problem of your own that is being expressed in terms of a dollar sign. You might also be pointing to your own insecurity about yourself or about your relationship with the dead person.

One form of reaction to death worth noting is displayed in the insistence on having the casket open so that the body may be on view. Morticians have become artists in "rejuvenating" the dead so that they often appear healthier-looking than they were in life. Several years ago I attended the funeral of a man I had known since boyhood. He had died after a long illness in which he wasted away. I was surprised, therefore, when I saw his body, for he was the picture of health, with a glow in his cheeks he never had when he was alive. Again I was surprised when a member of the family tapped me on the shoulder and said, "My, doesn't he look well? He looks like he is asleep." I began to wonder if this was not a kind of play-acting, a kind of collusion—probably unintentional—on the part of the undertaker and the family in an effort to deny that he was dead.

This kind of denial of death is bound up in the identity of the bereaved. The refusal to accept the fact that a person is gone, never to return, indicates that the mourner may be saying, among other things, that he cannot accept his own mortality—the fact that he, too, will die someday.

One of the most extreme reactions to death involves the grief of the person whose life has become so wrapped up in the existence of another that he cannot face the fact of the death of a loved one. This was the case with Sam Brewster when his Ella died after sixty-two years of marriage.

Ella and Sam had grown up together in a small New England town and had been inseparable throughout their lives. They remained in the town of their birth, rearing three children and becoming active in the community. In conversation, each made frequent reference to the other, and their friends and relatives usually referred to them as EllanSam, as though they were one name and one person.

Indeed, they were so much like two halves of the same body that their only separation during their marriage was a traumatic experience. Ella had to fly west for her brother's funeral. In the week she was gone, Sam was depressed and forlorn; he perked up only when he saw a tearful Ella step off an airplane.

No one was surprised, therefore, that when Ella died in her sleep of a heart attack, Sam was plunged into prolonged, deep mourning. Those close to him became concerned about his health. His children invited him to live with or near them, but he refused, remaining in his home and brooding. Finally Sam's depression became so deep that one of his friends summoned Sam's oldest son to try to cheer him up. Nothing would help.

"I know how much you miss Mom," the son told his father. "We all miss her a lot. We all loved her, too. But you can't go on this way. Why don't you take a trip or find something to do and pick up the pieces of your life?"

Sam was silent for a moment. Then he said, "She was my life, and now that life is finished."

Within a week, Sam was dead.

The separation caused by Ella's death had created problems that related to Sam's concept of himself. In a sense, he felt he *was* his wife. Perhaps if he had predeceased her, she would have reacted in much the same way, for theirs was a rare relationship of interdependence. In most cases, active grief runs its course, but what Sam experienced seemed to be more than either grief or sadness. His very being was threatened, almost as though one of his vital organs had been removed. Sam's sense of feeling alive depended on Ella's physical presence. In this sense he had never become a person in his own right, and so he could not cope with the sudden deprivation of the one who was his "life's blood."

The strange aspect of this was that Sam never recognized that he was dependent on Ella for his sense of identity. He always regarded himself as quite self-sufficient. In many ways he was, but deep inside he had never developed a sense of himself adequate enough to tide him over some of life's most critical moments. As long as Ella was at his side, he got along fine, but without her he was a cipher.

Another pronounced kind of grief that produces an identity crisis is far more common than that suffered by Sam Brewster. This is grief compounded by anger. Louise J. managed to weather such a crisis. Her grief came not from the loss of a mate, for she never married, but followed the death of her mother. The roots of Louise's identity crisis were planted in her late teens when her father died. Because her two sisters and brother already were married, she felt it her duty to remain at home to "keep Mother company." The least she could do, she felt, was to see that her mother was not alone at night.

Louise had friends and dated occasionally but never became seriously involved romantically. Every few years she took a long vacation with one or two of the girls at the office, but she devoted most of her time to her mother, an attentiveness that drew praise for her unselfish nature.

When I talked with Louise some years later, she observed that her "life with Mother" had seemed to pass quickly. And as the years sped by, she found that she spent more and more time caring for her mother, who had become an invalid. This restricted Louise increasingly, but it was a burden she bore with a keen attitude of devotion.

Inevitably her mother died. Louise, then in her fifties, felt disconsolate and alone—almost deserted. The passage of weeks and months brought no relief. Life had lost its purpose —and interest. Periodically Louise felt she could not go on living without her mother. However, instead of languishing into extinction, Louise decided to seek help. She talked with her doctor about her depression, thinking it might be physically induced. He referred her to me.

When she came into my office, she was very angry. Having been religious, she asked me how God could have taken away her mother who meant so much to her. As we talked, it became apparent why her mother had been so important in her life.

What Louise had interpreted as devotion—and what others had regarded as a high sense of duty—really was something else. Louise finally conceded that at times she resented "having" to stay at home with her mother. When I asked why she had not left, she acknowledged that she had been afraid to. The world seemed to be cruel and threatening. If she had not had her mother to advise her about what to do, she would not have known how to deal with many situations that had confronted her through the years. It was obvious that because Louise's concept of herself had never developed clearly, her mother's death left her with the feeling that she no longer could cope with life.

Sam and Louise present only two extremes to which grief carries people. For most of us the experience of losing someone dear through death is not quite so devastating, but it often does present a kind of identity crisis in our lives, whoever the loved one may be. This is to be expected, because separation through death is the most definitive and final of all separations. It is also one of the few absolutely irreversible experiences of life.

Of course it is normal to display genuine sorrow over the loss of someone close. Tears often provide a therapeutic way to "let out" grief. To try to inhibit our own or another's genuine sorrow is inappropriate. Grief is a process that must be worked through, and it often takes time. But we should distinguish between sorrow resulting from a sense of loss and destructive or pathological grief such as that of Sam and Louise.

What we experience as grief at the time of a death is generally a complex emotion or set of emotions. There is the aspect that can best be described as anger, which in turn has two principal facets: anger because someone we loved has been taken away and anger *at* a loved one for having left us. Illogical? Of course, but in the recesses of our unconscious we are quite often not logical. That still, small voice that speaks for the infant lurking in all of us is enraged at the loved one who has had the audacity to desert us.

The degree to which we are able to handle our anger—and *how* we handle it—is directly related to our development of our concept of ourselves. If this concept is swathed in the existence of another to the extent that we feel we can live only with and through him, then his death becomes a threat to our sense of being. Because we are threatened, we may become unreasonably angry toward the person who has left us. We may turn our anger on God, on other people, or on life in general.

For example, I knew a woman who seemed to be deeply religious—until gripped by tragedy. She had been a regular churchgoer and talked a lot about her faith. Then her entire attitude changed with the death of her small son, who was run over by an automobile. She became angry at God and the church, and soon her anger turned to hatred. Not only did she stop attending church services; she began to make comments such as "How could a loving God take my Freddie away?" Repeatedly she declared that nothing could heal her sorrow, which she had confused with devastation. Sorrow is a fitting response to death. But too often when our self-concept is shaky, we confuse grief with a personal devastation that does not permit us to go on. The feeling is that the death has happened to *us*. Instead of sorrowing because the dead person has been deprived of further life, we turn the tragedy in upon ourselves.

As I talked with this woman it became evident that she was experiencing not only genuine grief but something beyond. She had seen her little boy as so much of an extension of herself that her reasons for living were bound up in him. When he was killed, she felt that she, too, had perished. I was able to help her sort out the difference between herself and her son, between her sorrow and her devastation, between her loneliness and her feeling of being lost, but it was a long time before she was able to resume her life on a constructive plane.

The best safeguard against such a feeling of devastation is, of course, the cushion that is provided by a strong sense of self. It may help to bear in mind that in one sense everyone is alone. While we live in relation to others and with others, and many of these associations are meaningful, in the final analysis there is a core of our lives that must be lived alone. The separation caused by death can teach us whether we really can face life alone. No one can escape such a lesson at some time, for the day must inevitably come when death must separate us from others. Whether we learn from the lesson is another matter.

Facing a loss through death thus can be a constructive, although painful, experience. One of its constructive aspects is the fact that even though death separates us from a loved one, the memory of a deep relationship may have a lasting effect. Another aspect is the ability to accept the fact that someday we, too, will die. While the separation from a loved one certainly is an unhappy experience, the emotions of the relationship, the recollections, the experience live on. When George Bernard Shaw's wife died after forty years of marriage, he said that nothing, not even death, could destroy their relationship. They were physically separated, but what they were to one another could never end. A recent play containing searing dialogue about a variety of identity problems, *I Never Sang for My Father,* contains a line saying that death is a separation but it does not end a relationship, whether good or bad, loving or filled with hate. The memory does indeed linger on.

Acceptance of the fact that each of us is finite can help to make the death of someone close to us more acceptable. Unfortunately, our culture presents too many experiences that blind us to this. We have become too dear to our parents, our parents have become too dependent on us, and our children have become too dear to us. Our culture "implies" that if we accomplish certain goals, if we get to "the top," we will in a sense become our own gods. Quite clearly the implication is that if we become our own gods, we can control life and death. One is reminded of the parable Jesus told of the foolish rich man who thought he could arrange his life to make the future certain. God spoke to him one day, telling him that despite his well-laid plans for security he was going to die.

Probably no one is more aware of his mortality than the

young soldier. I learned this when I served in the Korean War.
I used to wonder how it was possible for men from our comfortable culture to face death from every side every day and
every night without fleeing in panic. Quite a few became ter-
ror-stricken, of course, and could not cope with the situation,
but most did not run away. There were moments when the
rest of us were terrified to the core. But most of the time the
men were able to carry out even the most hideous tasks without cringing at the thought of their own deaths.

I came to know these young men very well. As I talked with
them it became clear that they were able to live and do their
tasks day by day because they had learned to accept, even at
their rather tender ages, the fact that one day they would die,
whether on a muddy hill in Korea or in their beds at home.
They neither courted nor avoided death. They lived in the
hope that they would not be required to face the experience
under wartime conditions and at their young ages, but they
were able to accept the existence of death as an integral part
of life.

Samuel Johnson wrote that man is not afraid of death, but
of dying. I think many of the soldiers on the battlefield—as
well as great numbers of those who have never fired a shot in
their lives—come to share this belief.

Thus, how we deal with the prospect of our own deaths as
well as the deaths of others tells us a lot about ourselves and
about our culture.

We have spoken of prolonged grief, of grief compounded
by anger and resentment. There are other manifestations of
grief that are equally dynamic and destructive, as has been

mentioned. In addition there is the kind of grief that is masked in shock, and there is grief over missed opportunities.

One particular cause for anguish is guilt expressed through grief. Some people are guilty because they cannot or do not grieve. Some feel guilty because they think they have somehow shortchanged the person who has died, or because consciously or unconsciously they have wished this person dead.

There is also premature grief, as in the case of mourning for a relative or friend who has sunk so far into senility or a fatal illness that he is "dead" as the person he was. Grief for this person comes during his physical lifetime; his subsequent physical death is often a relief.

And then there is delayed grief, as in the case of a young woman I know. As a child, she was very close to her grandfather and spent a great deal of time with him. When he died, she did not show outward signs of grief and said later that she had not been able to bring herself to feel that he was really gone. The farm he owned remained in the family and served as a kind of link between her and her grandfather. A number of years after his death, the family sold the farm. It was only then that she broke down and cried real tears over her grandfather. This was the first sign of her grandfather's death that was real to her, and she went through the grief others had experienced after he died. Her grief was not unhealthy and it was short-lived.

There is still another rather subtle facet to the matter of death and grief. It may be that we tend more and more to segregate old people in nursing homes, retirement havens, and other Golden Age retreats as a way of dealing with the identity crisis that arises from the death of anyone close to us, which tells us as dramatically as possible that we too will die someday. By putting the old folks out of sight, we are able, at least to an extent, to put them out of mind while we turn to emphasizing youth and papering over the ultimate reality.

Death is as much a part of life as being born. How we face death, someone else's or our own, is a reflection of how we have dealt with the identity crises that have beset us throughout our lives. A well-balanced concept of who we are necessarily includes emotional as well as intellectual acceptance of the fact that, one day, our loved ones will leave us and that, on another day, we ourselves will die.

12

You Aren't Your Brother's Keeper

Tragedies produced by the identity crisis have paused at the doorsteps of nearly all of us. There is scarcely a family without at least one person who has some kind of mental or emotional difficulty. People with problems and problem people are with us all. Directly or indirectly we are involved, whether we actually do anything to help remedy the difficulties or not.

A mother learns to her horror that her son is a homosexual. A wife slowly comes to the painful realization that her husband has a severe drinking problem. Parents are puzzled when confronted with defiant teen-age children who go through a period in which they hold all adults in contempt and regard them as insufferably stupid. A child grows up and leaves home and cannot understand why his middle-aged mother becomes despondent and purposeless. Relatives gossip about the executive who works overtime at the office, apparently neglecting his wife. A grieving widower still has not put the pieces of his life back together months after his wife's death. Aged parents have become dependent and senile, and their children find themselves unable to accept them as irreversibly deteriorating.

Problems of this sort, as we have seen, confront us all, either directly or indirectly. Such manifestations of the identity crisis may actually be our own or those of a loved one, a dear friend, or a co-worker. One problem that often confronts—and even confounds—us is this: When the problem is not directly ours, what responsibility do we have? Is it enough to be able to understand the problem of a relative or a good friend? Or should we go beyond understanding? While we may not be qualified to give any objective or professional advice—although God knows there is an abundance to be had—should we inject ourselves into a situation even to the extent of suggesting a person seek help?

Naturally these questions are not easy to answer. So many variables come into play that to attempt any sweeping answers would be sheer folly. However, a good place to start is to ask ourselves: "Whose problem is it and how, if at all, does it relate to me?" When a son shows homosexual tendencies, whose problem is it? Is it his parents' or is it *his?* Who suffers most from the process of senility, the aggravated children or the aging parent? While it is natural for the problems of others to cause us discomfort and even suffering, we still need to distinguish sometimes between our own anguish and that of the person who actually has the problem.

A good example of this is the alcoholic. Certainly the misery he engenders touches many lives, particularly those of the people closest to him. But the problem with alcohol is still *his,* rather than that of his wife or children. To be more accurate, it is, in many instances, an indication of an emotional problem deep inside him. While it is true that the rest of us often suffer from the side effects, the problem basically belongs to the person who has it. In short, the drinking problem is in the last analysis the problem of the drinker; homosexuality is the problem of the homosexual, and senility is the problem of the senile. Our obligation is to try to determine where the problem lies, whether we ought to get involved in it, and if so, how.

Before a problem can be dealt with, whether within yourself or in someone close to you, it must be acknowledged to exist. It is amazing, even in this day of psychological enlightenment, how many people hide or cover up serious problems.

For an understanding of problems such as homosexuality, adultery, and alcoholism, it is necessary to cast off the secrecy that often still surrounds them and face them directly. Even today a lot of fear and concealment surround emotional problems. When it comes to admitting to oneself that a son is homosexual, a husband is a drunkard, or a wife is playing around, individuals still often feel embarrassed, defensive, frightened, and unable to cope. Amazingly, some people still have the idea that a person with an emotional problem is inferior and that his difficulty is somehow a reflection on *him*.

The truth is that no one is free from neurotic conflicts. Everyone has some emotional idiosyncrasy. While some of us are relatively free of severe conflict and others learn to handle personal quirks better than most, there still are many who are able to cope with them only up to a point and then find they cannot go further.

Once we face the fact that a problem exists, we can then ask to what degree we ought to become involved. First, we need to find out if the problem lies within ourselves. If it does, we should first of all learn not to be angry at ourselves for having a problem or to feel it is a sign of inferiority when we conclude we need assistance or guidance. On the contrary, such an admission, in addition to being the beginning of wisdom, is often a sign of strength. In awakening to a problem within someone else, the first and most important way we can help is through an understanding that the person probably has no control over the way he acts or feels. It is important also to recognize that you and he are different, separate individuals. This old but still valid principle of acceptance does not imply your tacit approval but rather communicates the fact that you are willing to accept a person even if he is faced with problems. Such an attitude in itself can be a great help to a troubled person, for it shows you have respect for him despite his difficulties.

In the case of a parent confronted with a problem child such as Joe, the boy discussed in Chapter 2, something clearly often can—and should—be done by the mother and father to obtain help for the youngster. There may be other times when it is advisable to suggest to someone close to you that he might be able to obtain professional assistance. This has to be done carefully and tactfully and with the knowledge that such a suggestion can have a positive effect only if you accept the person's right to reject it if he wishes.

Situations such as the following may warrant the mentioning of the availability of professional help:

• When a grieving person is unable to rebound in a reasonable period after such a traumatic event as the loss of a loved one.

• When there are sustained and prolonged periods of depression.

• When a person commits acts harmful to himself and others.

• When a person is unable to function in society, by holding a job, finishing a course in school, etc.

• When members of a family are consistently unable to communicate with or relate to one another.

Unfortunately, many people still hold the mistaken notion that a person must be severely disturbed to benefit from depth counseling or psychotherapy. This simply is not the case. In reality, it is appropriate to view such treatment as a way to educate the emotions—in much the same way the mind is educated in school. Depth counseling and psychotherapy are tools that can assist a person in living more completely by learning to experience and express himself more effectively.

When we reach a decision to suggest that a relative or friend seek professional assistance, we should do one more thing before we act. We should examine ourselves to determine whether and to what degree we may be motivated by a hope to avoid an irritating situation. How we approach a troubled person with the suggestion that he seek help will be determined in large part by our own reaction to his problem. The desire to be helpful in a crisis often springs from the fact that when we become aware of a deep-seated disturbance in

others, we become anxious or angry. We feel we must do
something to assuage our *own* discomfort. We often become
angry also at those who are ill. If we feel that "Jim could
straighten himself out if he would only get hold of things,"
the impatience implicit in this attitude is likely to be com-
municated to him in the way we make our suggestion. "Get
hold of yourself" is one of the favorite admonitions to someone gripped by an emotional upheaval. How absurd! If the
person could get hold of himself he would not need anyone
to tell him to. This form of anxiety in the would-be helper
frequently results from a lack of understanding; when we
don't understand things, we tend to become anxious or angry,
and we become much less able to deal with situations.

One good way to gauge your motives is to ask yourself:
How do I feel when my offer of help is rejected? Do I get angry? Do I feel that my own worth or self-concept somehow
has been diminished by this seeming rebuff? Do I give the
person the right to accept or reject the help I offer him?
Do I show him this much respect as a person? Do I really
accept the fact that in the final analysis I can take responsibility only for my own life? Sometimes we become so upset
by the problems of others that we get a little mixed up about
our own roles, thereby being unable to accept their right to
take or leave our counsel. This then becomes an identity
problem for us.

Here a distinction should be made, too, between being responsible *for* another person and having a responsibility *to*
him. A parent not only has a responsibility *to* his children, in
a sense, when they are too small to care for themselves, but
he also is responsible *for* them. However, at some point, a

child must take responsibility for himself. Likewise, the practitioner who treats a person has a responsibility to him without being responsible for him.

If your approach is inspired by genuine feelings of respect and love, your task will be easier and more acceptable. Bear in mind, too, that the person you are advising has rights and privileges. Coercion can be harmful to him, and treatment will be of little or no value unless *he* wants it. Therefore, accept the possibility that he will refuse to accept your guidance. He may be wrong, but it is his life and he has a right to accept or reject proposals of help—within limits, of course. There are times when the law and society say a person's freedom of choice must be curtailed for his and society's good. Self-destructive acts or violations of the rights of others are grounds in most states for removing people from society, regardless of how *they* may feel.

It cannot be repeated too often that you should *never, never, never* try to force your help on people. As a matter of fact, it really cannot be done. You may go as far as you can or wish in charity and concern for another human being, but offering help is one thing; demanding that a person accept it is another. The minute you make this demand, you are violating him as a person, and he *is* a person whatever his symptom or his plight. Too often we tend to equate people and their problems, but a human being is never the same as his problem; he is always much more. An example drawn from the world of medicine may help to illustrate this. When a doctor examines a patient suffering from an acutely inflamed appendix, he does not see the problem organ as the entire person. The patient may be preoccupied with his pain to the exclusion of every-

thing else, but the doctor does not see him as Mr. Appendi-
citis. He takes the entire person into account and considers
him in deciding how he will treat the painful area.

So a good part of the coping—not the curing—depends on
understanding. There is nothing wrong with helping another
human, but to make the demand of ourselves that we should
be able to help in every situation and to demand of another
person that he accept our help is a violation of both the individual and ourselves. Nobody is God and nobody should try
to play God.

Once a person decides to seek help, he should be encouraged to make his own appointment. Sometimes we try to do
too much for someone we love. If he decides to make his
own arrangements, he can demonstrate he is really motivated
to get help and, at the same time, he is able to maintain his
integrity in his own eyes. It is for such reasons that, except
in special instances, most therapists and treatment centers
refuse to make an appointment with anyone but the person
who is searching for help.

Naturally there are emergencies where immediate attention
is required without going through formalities and where there
is no time to carry out the self-help principle. In such cases,
a call to the nearest hospital will bring immediate help or
information as to where it can be obtained. The police in
larger cities can usually direct callers to sources of emergency
assistance.

In encouraging a person to get guidance, it is advisable
to be able also to suggest where he should go. There are several kinds of treatment facilities and there are private practitioners equipped to deal with various types of problems. In

the past, emotional difficulties were treated mainly by psychiatrists and psychologists, but recently clinically trained social workers, pastoral counselors, marriage counselors, and other experts have entered the picture. Regardless of the profession, many of those engaged in helping people sort out their emotional lives are trained in depth understanding of the problems. Those in private practice often retain psychiatrists and psychologists as consultants.

The family physician and clergyman are good sources for information on where to obtain treatment. School guidance counselors and psychologists often know where help can be found. Judges, lawyers, mental health associations, and social agencies also may have lists of clinical services. Most agencies are listed in the telephone book, and mental health clinics are listed officially in states where licensing of such facilities is required. The National Institute of Mental Health has published the names and addresses of all licensed mental health clinics in the country in a booklet that can be obtained by sending sixty cents to the Superintendent of Documents, Government Printing Office, Washington, D.C. 20402.

With the rise of pastoral counseling as a specialty, and in light of the fact that many people take their emotional problems to their clergymen, several hundred pastoral counseling centers are now operating across the country. These services offer counseling by clinically trained clergymen who work in consultation with psychiatrists and psychologists. Many of the clergymen are trained as psychotherapists as well. A list of these centers can be obtained by writing the American Association of Pastoral Counselors, 201 East 19th Street, New York City, New York 10003.

Other organizations that may be of help in providing names of services and practitioners include Psychiatric Outpatient Centers of America, P.O. Box 1048, Oil City, Pennsylvania 16301, and the American Association of Marriage Counselors, Inc., 3620 Maple Avenue, Dallas, Texas 75219.

Hospitals in some of the larger cities now maintain walk-in services for emotional emergencies at which anyone can receive treatment without being hospitalized unless there is a serious crisis. Some hospitals and other centers have suicide prevention services, with staff members on duty twenty-four hours a day to receive those who walk in and to deal with those who telephone. With the increasing emphasis on community mental health programs, more services of this kind will be available in the future.

There are times when it is advisable to refer a person in crisis to a service, agency, or organization that is not directly involved in providing psychological or medical help. The best-known of these is, of course, Alcoholics Anonymous. Almost every town of any size has a chapter whose members are always on call to help other alcoholics. More recently, two other supportive organizations have been established—Gamblers Anonymous and Weight Watchers. Those who join these groups become aware that a large part of their problem is emotional. By being with others who have the same problems or similar ones, there is an element of mutual sympathy and motivation in overcoming at least some of the symptoms. Another group that operates in much the same way is Synanon, which helps people out of narcotics addiction through a kind of group therapy program. Parents Without Partners is an organization composed of the widowed and divorced that helps them to find new lives or at least adjust to living without their spouses.

These are some of the things you *can* recommend if you feel that a situation warrants giving others encouragement to seek help. However, there are times when such direct intervention is *not* called for. Rather, it becomes necessary sometimes to learn how to live *with* other people's identity problems, and by doing that, you may assist them in beginning to seek solutions for themselves; at least the strain on all concerned will be minimized.

Many difficult questions arise in situations in which individuals have snarled their lives and made things unpleasant for others. If not the most difficult, one of the more important considerations is *how to go about trying to live with other people's problems* and still maintain a sense of your own identity. Where do you fit in their identity crises? When is your help needed and when should you remain apart? For example, the misery suffered by many homosexuals may create some unhappiness for others as well. The so-called innocent bystanders may be the very people who have contributed to the fact that a person is a deviate from sexual normalcy—but it still is not *their* problem, nor can they solve it. They can hope to do a great deal if they try to understand the homosexual; since people do not grow in a vacuum it might help them to a better understanding of homosexuality if they tried to determine the role they might have played in the onset of the problem.

In all crises, it is important that we understand and accept the fact that we *never* really know what another person is experiencing. We can have an idea, an approximation, but we can never know precisely what the other person is enjoying or suffering at any particular time, be it husband, wife, child, or friend. You can point to a family and say, "Now, *there* is a happy home!" when all the time they may be miserable. A father may boast that "Ours is a wonderful, fine, happy family," when underneath there may be rumblings of real tragedy. The person who *supposes* that another is happy draws his inference from what he knows culturally and the experiences he himself has had. In this, he may or may not be correct since feelings are so very personal. And even if you guess correctly when you say so-and-so is happy, you cannot know what happiness actually means to him.

Now the fact that you indeed are not required to be your brother's keeper certainly does not mean that you should turn your back on the person in trouble. You can often give support, but in doing so, you should take care not to present yourself as a savior. In other words, instead of imposing your helpfulness on another, sometimes the most you can do is learn to live with his problem. This in itself can, in some instances, give him the support he needs.

Sometimes we become frightened or feel threatened when confronted with another's problems, particularly those of the aged parent who becomes senile. It may be because we do not understand what is happening that we become frightened and upset. We may resent having to deal with such a person. At the same time, our resentment may spring from fear that someday we will be in similar straits, withering away as we await death.

Becoming "frightened" or "threatened" means that when

we see a problem in another person it creates in us a realization not only that we may be in a similar plight someday but also that something we had is being taken away. Sometimes we feel threatened when we are deprived of something we want or when we realize that we have a need that will not be fulfilled. We feel threatened also if we do not understand, if something remains mysterious. What is unknown often scares all of us. We become anxious. Life grows tedious and tortuous.

How often have you heard a mother react to a tragic occurrence in a family by crying, "Why did this happen to *me?*" She may say this when she learns her son is in jail, when she is widowed, or when her husband loses one job after another. Taking an objective view, we may wonder why she takes it so personally. Isn't it possible she is really talking about *herself* and her own problems of development? While we may understand her disappointment or discomfort, we are justified in wondering why she sees it as happening to her directly. Isn't she perhaps really saying that she is still at an immature stage of development where she feels everything that happens is in direct relation to her and perhaps even because of her? Isn't it also possible that she is expressing fear and guilt about the possibility she may in some way have been the cause of the problem? In other words, when she says, "Why did this happen to me?" she may actually mean, "What did I do that was wrong?" In reacting to another person's problems this way, she may be dealing with her own identity problem by taking the attitude that things that are happening to others somehow are unduly influenced by her.

The person with this reaction may be avoiding any real